BRITISH
and
AMERICAN
POETRY

BRITISH
and
AMERICAN
POETRY

HERBERT CHURCH, Jr.

St. Paul's School

Concord,

New Hampshire

Independent School Press

Wellesley Hills   Massachusetts

CONTENTS

TO THE STUDENT

The purpose of this book is to give you a basic knowledge of the chronology of British and American poetry, from the ballads and Chaucer to Frost and Eliot. After you have finished, you should be familiar with the names of literary periods and their approximate dates, authors within those periods, and well-known poems by those authors.

We are concerned, then, with a *chronological* or *historical* approach to poetry. In addition to learning names of major poets and poems you should learn that poets are products of their times. They were differently gifted; but they used their gifts to write as they did, on the subjects they chose, in considerable measure because of the times they lived in. Poetry is obviously related to other kinds of writing; less obviously it is also related to the other arts. There is a real relationship between what (and how) poets wrote at a given time and what they painted, how they dressed, what they built, how they amused themselves, and what music they listened to. It is hoped that you will begin to see this relationship.

I

THE ORIGINS OF ENGLISH

European literary figures occasionally dismiss English as a "mongrel" language. While every language to some extent borrows from others, the descent of a relatively "pure" language like French can be traced century by century from its Latin ancestor. English, on the other hand, is a mixture of two quite dissimilar linguistic strains: the "Romance" (chiefly Norman and Angevin French) and the Anglo-Saxon (related to German and Scandinavian). If one result of this union is the unfortunate complexity of English spelling, two happy results are the simplicity of English grammar and the richness of English vocabulary.[1] Since there could be no English poetry without English, a brief history of our language is in order.

When Julius Caesar attempted to invade Britain, he found there a Celtic people speaking a language not unlike that of the Gauls. Britain (excluding Scotland and Ireland) became a Roman province and remained one for several hundred years, but the Latin language made little headway. There are impressive Roman remains of a physical sort, but when Roman power was withdrawn in the fourth century, the language of the people was still "British."

The partly Christian, Celtic, ex-Roman island was assaulted in the fifth and sixth centuries by a very different kind of invader. Unlike the Romans, who governed but seldom settled, the Anglo-Saxons came with their families, to stay. They were a pagan folk, living in what is now southern Denmark and the adjacent parts of Germany, and speaking various Germanic dialects. They may themselves have been fleeing invaders from points further east, such as the Huns; whatever their reasons for coming, they apparently preferred eastern and southern England to their old homeland. Some of the original Celtic inhabitants were absorbed into the new Anglo-Saxon kingdoms; others fled west to Wales and Cornwall or (to a lesser extent) north to Scotland, where (par-

---

1. There are thousands of Romance and Anglo-Saxon equivalents in modern English; hence its wealth of synonyms.

1

ticularly in Wales) languages akin to the original Celtic (Gaelic/Gallic) are still spoken.[2]

Christianity, present in Roman Britain, was re-introduced into the north of England from Ireland early in the sixth century, and into the south by St. Augustine of Canterbury at the end of the century. In 664 it was agreed at the Synod of Whitby that the two branches should merge and accept the Papacy, which had sent Augustine on his mission. England ("Angle-Land") was first a patchwork of numerous Anglo-Saxon states; these gradually merged into four main kingdoms: Northumbria (in the northeast), Mercia (in the midlands), Anglia (east of London), and Wessex ("West Saxony"—south of the Thames). When Danish invaders in the eighth and ninth centuries temporarily crushed Northumbria, Wessex became the most important. Here lived Alfred, the greatest Anglo-Saxon King (871-901), a patron of learning and of the arts who was responsible for the survival of much Anglo-Saxon literature.

Although the Anglo-Saxons contributed roughly half the content of standard English—and the more common half— their language, usually called "Old English," is for us a thoroughly foreign tongue. Not even the alphabet is entirely familiar. The great literary monument of Old English is *Beowulf,* an epic poem by an unknown author. It dates from around 700. The author was a Northumbrian and possibly a Christian, but the poem, set in Denmark and southern Sweden, deals with the pagan past. Basically, it is a typical heroic tale of a larger-than-life hero who lives in a world of monsters and dragons. It is told with great skill, however, and some of the poetic devices used have rather recently found their way back into English.

In 1066 England was invaded for the last time, William of Normandy defeating King Harold at the Battle of Hastings. Though the Normans, as their name would indicate, were descended from Norsemen who had long before occupied northern France, by the eleventh century they had become thoroughly French in language and civilization. They provided the Romance partner in the linguistic union that gave birth to the English language.

For a considerable time after the Conquest, French and Old English existed side by side, the conquerors speaking the former, the conquered the latter. Gradually the distinction between Norman and Saxon became blurred. After several generations the Normans and Angevins began to think of England as home, although they still retained

---

2. Brittany in France is somewhat analagous to Wales. It is said that Breton fishermen can communicate in vestiges of their ancient tongue with Welsh-speaking Welshmen.

substantial possessions in France and moved freely from one country to the other. In the year 1200, King John of England was also Duke of Normandy, Gascony, and Aquitaine, Count of Anjou and Maine, and overlord of the Duchy of Brittany. He controlled more of France than the French King, whose struggles to assert his supremacy pushed Norman and Saxon together. It is worth noting that the early Kings of England after the Conquest had virtually no English blood: William the Conqueror's wife claimed descent from Alfred the Great, but William himself had no English blood and his immediate successors made their marriages (often very profitable political "deals") in France. Nevertheless, political, social and economic mixing developed continuously between the subject English and their foreign rulers.

Not too surprisingly, a linguistic blend developed. We refer to it as "Middle English," and for all its oddities it is no longer a foreign language to us. In 1362 it became the official language of Parliament and the Royal Law Courts.

Some time prior to this date, the first Middle English poem of which we have record was written. A charming little song in praise of the springtime, it appears below, alongside a word-by-word paraphrase.

	Sumer is icumen in;	Summer is coming in;	
	Lhude sing, cuccu!	Loudly sing, cuckoo!	
	Groweth sed, and bloweth med,	Grows seed and blooms meadow,	
	And springth the wude nu.	And springs the wood now.	
5	Sing, cuccu!	Sing, cuckoo!	5
	Awe bleteth after lomb,	Ewe bleats after lamb,	
	Lhouth after calve cu;	Lows after calf cow;	
	Bulluc sterteth, bucke verteth;	Bullock frisks, buck hides in the green;	
	Murie sing, cuccu!	Merrily sing, cuckoo!	
10	Cuccu! cuccu!	Cuckoo! cuckoo!	10
	Wel singes thu, cucco;	Well sing you, cuckoo;	
	Ne swik thu naver nu.	Never cease you now.	

Written about 1275, the "Cuckoo Song" is linguistically interesting as well as poetically delightful. Two signs of the merging of French and Old English might be noted: (1) *verteth* (line 8)—a French root with an English ending; and (2) the French double negative form in the last line with the English *naver* substituted for the French *jamais*.

II

THE POPULAR BALLADS

Although the language of England and most of Lowland Scotland was English by the fourteenth century, the native tongue was not always the medium of literature. Because Latin continued to be the universal language of scholarship, it was used for most serious writing; and courtly circles continued to use French, largely because it remained the common language of the European upper classes, who, in the days before the concepts of nationalism and patriotism developed, and in the days when large numbers of people still joined together on pilgrimages and crusades, mingled more freely and closely than they have ever done since. As we look back on the late medieval period in Britain, we note that the two finest works of the time were in English—Chaucer's *Canterbury Tales* (begun, 1387) and Sir Thomas Malory's *Morte Darthur* (1470).[1] In their own time, though, these may well have appeared to be exceptions to the notion that English was not a literary language. It was, however, unquestionably the language of popular literature, the dominant form of which was the ballad.

Ballads are still written today; an American classic is "Frankie and Johnnie." In late medieval times, however, before general literacy, they were the most important form of popular entertainment. Hundreds of them were written; and because they weren't usually literally "written," but passed on orally, many versions of the more popular ones appeared. The fifteenth century was the great era for ballads, but very few were written down that early. It wasn't actually until 1765 that there was a systematic and scholarly ballad collection made (Thomas Percy, *Reliques of Ancient English Poetry*); perhaps the definitive collection is that of Francis J. Child in the late nineteenth century.

Much nonsense has been put forth about the origins of ballads. In some mystic way an entity called "the folk" has been said to have produced them, and a great deal has been made of their crudity and

---

1. Malory's work, being prose, will not be dealt with; but it is noted among other things as the last important English book to be written before the printing press, and one of the first to be printed. William Caxton printed it in 1485.

primitive qualities. On the contrary, the most cursory look at the text of most ballads ought to convince a reader that these poems were written by poets who may have been anonymous but who certainly were competent, and whose poems may have been simple but certainly were neither crude nor primitive.

Ballads are easily recognized. Because they are meant to be memorized and sung, or at least recited to a musical accompaniment, their poetic form is strong and simple. A common stanza is a quatrain with four stresses on the first and third lines, three on the second and fourth, and a rhyme scheme *abcb* ("Sir Patrick Spens"). Also common is a refrain, particularly one which changes slightly each time it appears, thereby advancing the story ("Edward," "Lord Randal"). This technique is called "incremental repetition."

Ballads are stories above all else; they tell their tale with vigor and economy. There is very little explanatory material, and the author tends to keep himself out of his narrative. The subjects are highly dramatic: warfare (particularly warfare between Scotland and England: hence the name Border Ballads), death, love, hate, treachery, the miraculous.

Poetry almost always suffers when not read aloud; ballads suffer more than most poems. A good ballad competently sung to one of the many traditional ballad melodies should convince anyone that the popular need not be second-rate.

SIR PATRICK SPENS

The king sits in Dumferling toune,
    Drinking the blude-reid wine:
"O whar will I get a guid sailor
    To sail this schip of mine?"

Up and spak an eldern knicht,   5
    Sat at the kings richt kne:
"Sir Patrick Spens is the best sailor
    That sails upon the se."

The king has written a braid[1] letter
    And signd it wi his hand,   10
And sent it to Sir Patrick Spens,
    Was walking on the sand.

The first line that Sir Patrick red,
    A loud lauch lauched he;
The next line that Sir Patrick red   15
    The teir blinded his ee.

"O wha is this has don this deid,
    This ill deid don to me,
To send me out this time o' the yeir,
    To sail upon the se!   20

"Mak haste, mak haste, my mirry men all,
    Our guid schip sails the morne."
"O say na sae,[2] my master deir,
    For I feir a deadlie storme.

"Late, late yestreen[3] I saw the new moone,   25
    Wi the auld moone in hir arme,
And I feir, I feir, my deir master,
    That we will cum to harme."

O our Scots nobles wer richt laith[4]
    To weet their cork-heild schoone;   30
Bot lang owre a' the play wer playd,
    Thair hats they swam aboone.[5]

1. broad   4. loath
2. so   5. above
3. yesterday evening

O lang, lang may their ladies sit,
  Wi thair fans into their hand,
Or eir they se Sir Patrick Spens   35
  Cum sailing to the land.

O lang, lang may the ladies stand,
  Wi thair gold kems in their hair,
Waiting for thair ain deir lords,
  For they'll se thame na mair.   40

Haf owre, haf owre to Aberdour,
  It's fiftie fadom deip,
And thair lies guid Sir Patrick Spens,
  Wi the Scots lords at his feit.

GET UP AND BAR THE DOOR

It fell about the Martinmass time,
  And a gay time it was then,
When our goodwife got puddings to make,
  And she's boild them in the pan.

The wind sae cauld blew south and north,   5
  And blew into the floor;
Quoth our goodman to our goodwife,
  "Gae out and bar the door."

"My hand is in my hussyfskap,[6]
  Goodman, as ye may see;   10
An[7] it shoud nae be barrd this hundred year,
  It's no be barrd for me!"

They made a paction tween them twa,
  They made it firm and sure,
That the first word whaeer[8] shoud speak, 15
  Shoud rise and bar the door.

---

6. housework   8. whoever
7. if

Then by there came two gentlemen,
    At twelve oclock at night,
And they could neither see house nor hall,
    Nor coal nor candle-light.   20

"Now whether is this a rich man's house,
    Or whether it is a poor?"
But neer a word would ane o them speak,
    For barring of the door.

And first they ate the white puddings,   25
    And then they ate the black;
Tho muckle[9] thought the goodwife to hersel,
    Yet neer a word she spake.

Then said the one unto the other,
    "Here, man, tak ye my knife;   30
Do ye tak aff the auld man's beard,
    And I'll kiss the goodwife."

"But there's nae water in the house,
    And what shall we do than?"
"What ails ye at the pudding-broo,   35
    That boils into the pan?"

O up then started our goodman,
    An angry man was he:
"Will ye kiss my wife before my een,
    And scad me wi pudding-bree?"   40

Then up and started our goodwife,
    Gied three skips on the floor:
"Goodman, you've spoken the foremost word,
    Get up and bar the door!'

---

9.   much

EDWARD

"Why dois your brand[10] sae drap wi bluid,
                 Edward, Edward,
Why dois your brand sae drap wi bluid,
   And why sae sad gang[11] ye O?"
"O I hae killed my hauke sae guid,
                 Mither, mither,
O I hae killed my hauke sae guid,
   And I had nae mair bot hee O."

"Your haukis bluid was nevir sae reid,
                 Edward, Edward   10
Your haukis bluid was nevir sae reid,
   My deir son I tell thee O."
"O I hae killed my reid-roan steid,
                 Mither, mither,
O I hae killed my reid-roan steid,   15
   That erst[12] was sae fair and frie O."

"Your steid was auld, and ye hae gat mair,
                 Edward, Edward,
Your steid was auld, and ye hae gat mair,
   Sum other dule[13] ye drie[14] O."   20
"O I hae killed my fadir deir,
                 Mither, mither,
O I hae killed my fadir deir,
   Alas, and wae is mee O!"

"And whatten penance wul ye drie for that,   25
                 Edward, Edward,
And whatten penance wul ye drie for that?
   My deir son, now tell me O."
"Ile set my feit in yonder boat,
                 Mither, mither,   30
Ile set my feit in yonder boat,
   And Ile fare ovir the sea O."

---

10. sword
11. go
12. formerly

13. grief
14. suffer

"And what wul ye doe wi your towirs and your ha,
              Edward, Edward,
And what wul ye doe wi your towirs and your ha,   35
   That were sae fair to see O?"
"Ile let thame stand tul they doun fa,
              Mither, mither,
Ile let thame stand tul they doun fa,
   For here nevir mair maun[15] I bee O."   40

"And what wul ye leive to your bairns and your wife,
              Edward, Edward,
And what wul ye leive to your bairns and your wife,
   Whan ye gang ovir the sea O?"
"The warldis room, late[16] them beg thrae life,   45
              Mither, mither,
The warldis room, late them beg thrae life,
   For thame nevir mair wul I see O."

"And what wul ye leive to your ain mither deir,
              Edward, Edward   50
And what wul ye leive to your ain mither deir?
   My deir son, now tell me O."
The curse of hell frae me sall ye beir,
              Mither, mither,
"The curse of hell frae me sall ye beir,
   Sic[17] counseils ye gave to me O."

LORD RANDAL

"O where hae ye been, Lord Randal, my son?
O where hae ye been, my handsome young man?"
"I hae been to the wild wood; mother, make my bed soon,
For I'm weary wi' hunting, and fain wald lie down."

"Where gat ye your dinner, Lord Randal, my son?   5
Where gat ye your dinner, my handsome young man?"
"I dined wi' my true-love; mother, make my bed soon,
For I'm weary wi' hunting, and fain wald lie down."

---

15.   must   17.   such
16.   let

"What gat ye to your dinner, Lord Randal, my son?
What gat ye to your dinner, my handsome young man?"   10
"I gat eels boil'd in broo; mother, make my bed soon,
For I'm weary wi' hunting, and fain wald lie down."

"What became of your bloodhounds, Lord Randal, my son?
What became of your bloodhounds, my handsome young man-"
"O they swell'd and they died; mother, make my bed soon,   15
For I'm weary wi' hunting, and fain wald lie down."

"O I fear ye are poison'd, Lord Randal, my son!
O I fear ye are poison'd, my handsome young man!"
"O yes! I am poison'd; mother, make my bed soon,
For I'm sick at the heart, and I fain wald lie down."   20

THE CHERRY-TREE CAROL

Joseph was an old man,
   and an old man was he,
When he wedded Mary
   in the land of Galilee.

Joseph and Mary walked   5
   through an orchard good,
Where was cherries and berries,
   so red as any blood.

Joseph and Mary walked
   through an orchard green,   10
Where was berries and cherries,
   as thick as might be seen.

O then bespoke Mary,
   so meek and so mild:
"Pluck me one cherry, Joseph,   15
   for I am with child."

O then bespoke Joseph:
   with words most unkind:
"Let him pluck thee a cherry
   that brought thee with child."   20

O then bespoke the babe,
    within his mother's womb:
"Bow down then the tallest tree,
    for my mother to have some."

Then bowed down the highest tree   25
    unto his mother's hand;
Then she cried, "See, Joseph,
    I have cherries at command."

O then bespoke Joseph:
    "I have done Mary wrong;   30
But cheer up, my dearest,
    and be not cast down."

Then Mary plucked a cherry,
    as red as the blood,
Then Mary went home   35
    with her heavy load.

Then Mary took her babe,
    and sat him on her knee,
Saying, "My dear son, tell me
    what this world will be."   40

"O I shall be as dead, mother,
    as the stones in the wall;
O the stones in the streets, mother,
    shall mourn for me all.

"Upon Easter-Day, mother,   45
    my uprising shall be;
O the sun and the moon, mother,
    shall both rise with me."

THE TWA CORBIES

As I was walking all alane,
I heard twa corbies[18] making a mane;[19]
The tane unto the t'other say,
"Where sall we gang and dine today?"

---

18. ravens   19. moan

"In behint yon auld fail[20] dyke,   5
I wot there lies a new-slain knight;
And naebody kens that he lies there,
But his hawk, his hound, and lady fair.

"His hound is to the hunting gane,
His hawk to fetch the wild-fowl hame,   10
His lady's ta'en another mate,
So we may mak our dinner sweet.

"Ye'll sit on his white hause-bane,[21]
And I'll pick out his bonny blue een;
Wi ae lock o' his gowden hair   15
We'll theek[22] our nest when it grows bare.

"Mony a one for him makes mane,
But nane sall ken where he is gane;
O'er his white banes when they are bare,
The wind sall blaw for evermair."   20

---

20. turf
21. neck-bone
22. thatch

III

GEOFFREY CHAUCER (c. 1340-1400)

Chaucer was by an overwhelming margin the supreme poet to write in Middle English. After almost 600 years he still ranks high, and a good case can be made that no major figure since is as much fun to read. He united to an extraordinary degree narrative skill, poetic technique, and a warm, humorous, tolerant literary personality.

A fair amount is known about Chaucer's life. He was a person of some consequence. Of mercantile family, he married into the lesser nobility and apparently enjoyed the confidence of important people at court, especially after John of Gaunt, Duke of Lancaster, the most powerful man in the Kingdom, married his mistress, Katharine Swynford, Chaucer's sister-in-law. Chaucer was sent on several confidential governmental missions, one of which took him as far as Italy. (Boccaccio provided a model for *The Canterbury Tales.*) As overseer of the customs service of the port of London he had the opportunity to travel widely in eastern England and to observe and meet all kinds of people. He himself went on a pilgrimage to Canterbury. In late medieval times, when most people traveled but little, there must have been few Englishmen who had traveled further and seen more than Goeffrey Chaucer.

Although Chaucer's literary output was considerable ("Troylus and Cryseyde," a tale of the Trojan War, should be mentioned), he is properly best known for his masterpiece, *The Canterbury Tales.* The "plot" hardly exists: 29 people en route to the shrine of St. Thomas à Becket meet at the Tabard Inn across the Thames from London. The inn-keeper suggests that the travelers relieve the monotony of their journey by telling each other stories. Each is to tell two tales on the way out and two on the way back; the teller of the best tale will be rewarded with a free dinner after the pilgrimage.

Begun about 1387, the work is unfinished. Instead of the 116 tales planned, there are but 23. They vary considerably in interest for the modern reader; there are, for example, long discussions of the problems of chivalry, which doubtless appealed more to Chaucer's immediate audience than to his present one. Perhaps because there were so few other diversions, writers in the Middle Ages showed an indefatigable interest in the details of dress, of chivalry, and of hunting etiquette that is best illustrated in the Middle English poem *Sir Gawayn and the Grene Knyght* and is also apparent throughout Chaucer's work.

Almost all the tales have some interest, however, and some are classics of their kind. Chaucer runs the gamut of human emotion but is not at his best with the heroic or tragic; his specialty is a kind of earthy ribaldry reminiscent of the comedies of Aristophanes. Perhaps even better than the tales themselves are Chaucer's brilliant profiles of the pilgrims ("Prologue") and his narrative interludes that tie the various tales together. The conversation of the voyagers is anything but solemn.

Most of the book is in *heroic couplets*—ten syllable iambic lines with the rhyme scheme aabbccdd, etc. There are several exceptions: some tales are in *rhyme royal* (iambic pentameter, seven line stanzas, ababbcc); there are two (very tedious) stories in prose.

Heroic couplets are rather easy to write but hard to write well. They tend to become monotonous in unskilled hands; further, the requirement of an end rhyme to each line can lead to a stop in the narrative at that point. Chaucer makes his couplets flow with the smoothness of unrhymed verse; he is helped by the frequency of the final *e* in Middle English, which gives him a softness at the end of the line lacking in modern English couplets. For example, the first two lines of the poem actually end in a *feminine rhyme:*

When that Aprille, with his shoures soote,
The droghte of March hath perced to the roote. . . .

The final *e* of *soote* and *roote* is pronounced—about as much as the *en* in *taken*. There is no punctuation after *roote,* and Chaucer's soft rhyme lets the reader move at once to the third line. If the word were the modern *root,* on the other hand, with its abrupt *masculine rhyme,* the reader would find it difficult to keep going.

For all its charm, the transitional Middle English presents enough of a vocabulary problem to be an obstacle to the enjoyment of Chaucer. The sections in this anthology are in the original form, since only a brief taste of Chaucer is given; those who wish to read further might well consult one of the modern "translations" available.

The justification of a "translation" is the fact that there is more to Chaucer than the charm of his verse. As was mentioned above, he knew his age well, and *The Canterbury Tales* is both a series of good stories and a marvelous (and rather surprising) picture of late medieval life.

Perhaps the first surprise is the good humor and gaiety that pervade all. The travelers are on a religious pilgrimage, but there is nothing grim or even solemn about their actions. In addition, there is a social tolerance unusual even in our day. Though there is a wide class distinction between the knight, the merchants, and the abbot, on the one hand, and the miller, the yeoman, and the cook, on the other, Chaucer never suggests that such social mixing is unusual. *The Canterbury Tales* are an excellent rebuttal of the old cliches about medieval rigidity and harshness.

Other surprises exist. The yeoman by definition is a commoner of low rank, yet he is a walking arsenal, from his "mighty bowe" to his "gay daggere." If his armed condition suggests the melancholy truth that the roads were not too safe in the time of Richard II, it also suggests a certain stability in the kingdom: not everywhere were peasants allowed to carry arms. Another surprise is the Wife of Bath. Chaucer uses a certain hyperbole in describing her (she had buried five husbands, for example), and hence we need not assume that a medieval woman typically would have been to Jerusalem and Rome; but her well-traveled status argues for rather less stagnation than we think of in our conception of the medieval.

Finally, Chaucer's gallery of characters gives flesh and blood to a number of bare facts that we note in history books. We are told that the Church entered into every aspect of life; we see that about one third of the party are directly connected with the Church. We know that this was the time of the Black Death; a doctor is a respected member of the group. The Monk, the Friar, and the Pardoner are living examples of the ecclesiastical abuses that were to bring on the Reformation; the Parson, who taught "Cristes loore and his apostles twelve," but "first he folwed it hymselve," shows the nobler side of the Church. The gentle nun, whom Chaucer applauds (with a bit of irony) for her good table manners, unconsciously displays one of the uglier aspects of medieval (and contemporary) Christendom when she tells her story of the good little boy whose throat is cut in the Jewish Ghetto because he innocently sings a Christian hymn on his way to school.

GEOFFREY CHAUCER (c. 1340-1400)

FROM THE PROLOGUE TO *THE CANTERBURY TALES*

When that Aprille with his shoures soote[1]
The droghte of March hath perced to the roote
And bathed every veyne in swich[2] licour
Of which vertu engendred is the flour;
When Zephirus eek[3] with his sweete breeth   5
Inspired hath in every holt and heeth
The tendre croppes, and the yonge sonne
Hath in the Ram his halve cours yronne,[4]
And smale foweles maken melodye,
That slepen al the nyght with open ye   10
(So priketh[5] hem nature in hir corages[6]),
Thanne longen folk to goon on pilgrimages,
And palmeres for to seken straunge strondes,
To ferne halwes,[7] kowthe[8] in sondry londes
And specially from every shires ende   15
Of Engelond to Caunterbury they wende,
The hooly blisful martir[9] for to seke,
That them hath holpen when that they were seeke.

Bifil that in that seson on a day,
In Southwerk at the Tabard as I lay   20
Redy to wenden on my pilgrymage
To Caunterbury with ful devout corage,
At nyght was come into that hostelrye
Wel nyne and twenty in a compaignye,
Of sondry folk, by aventure yfalle   25
In felaweshipe, and pilgrimes were they alle,
That toward Caunterbury wolden ryde.
The chambres and the stables weren wyde,
And wel we weren esed atte beste.[10]
And shortly, when the sonne was to reste,   30
So hadde I spoken with hem everichon[11]
That I was of hir felaweshipe anon,
And made forward erly for to ryse,
To take oure wey ther as I yow devyse.

1.	sweet	7.	distant saints
2.	such	8.	famous
3.	also	9.	Becket
4.	run (past participle)	10.	accomodated in the best way
5.	urges	11.	everyone
6.	dispositions		

But nathelees, whil I have tyme and space,   35
Er that I ferther in this tale pace,
Me thynketh it acordaunt to resoun
To telle yow al the condicioun
Of ech of hem, so as it semed me,
And whiche they weren, and of what degree,   40
And eek in what array that they were inne;
And at a knyght then wol I first bigynne.

  A KNYGHT ther was, and that a worthy man,
That fro the tyme that he first bigan
To riden out, he loved chivalrie,   45
Trouthe and honour, fredom and curtesie.
Ful worthy was he in his lordes werre,[12]
And therto[13] hadde he riden, no man ferre,[14]
As wel in cristendom as in hethenesse,
And evere honoured for his worthynesse.   50
At Alisaundre he was when it was wonne.
Ful ofte tyme he hadde the bord bigonne[15]
Aboven alle nacions in Pruce;
In Lettow hadde he reysed[16] and in Ruce,
No Cristen man so ofte of his degree.   55
In Gernade at the seege eek hadde he be
Of Algezir, and riden in Belmarye.
At Lyeys was he and at Satalye,
When they were wonne; and in the Grete See
At many a noble armee[17] hadde he be.   60
At mortal batailles hadde he been fiftene,
And foughten for oure feith at Tramyssene
In lystes thries, and ay slayn his foo.
This ilke[18] worthy knyght hadde been also
Somtyme with the lord of Palatye   65
Agayn[19] another hethen in Turkye.
And everemoore he hadde a sovereyn prys,[20]
And though that he were worthy, he was wys,
And of his port[21] as meeke as is a mayde.
He nevere yet no vileynye ne sayde   70
In al his lyf unto no maner wight.
He was a verray, parfit gentil knyght.
But, for to tellen yow of his array,
His hors were goode, but he was nat gay.

---

12. war, service   17. expedition
13. in addition   18. same
14. farther   19. against
15. sat at the head of the table   20. high praise
16. campaigned   21. bearing

Of fustian[22] he wered a gypon[23]   75
Al bismotered with his habergeon,[24]
For he was late ycome from his viage,
And wente for to doon his pilgrymage.

   With hym ther was his sone, a yong SQUIER,
A lovyere and a lusty bacheler,   80
With lokkes crulle[25] as they were leyd in presse.
Of twenty yeer of age he was, I gesse.

            *   *   *   *   *   *

   A YEMAN[26] hadde he and servants namo
At that tyme, for hym liste ride so;[27]
And he was clad in cote and hood of grene.   85
A sheef of pecok arwes, bright and kene,
Under his belt he bar ful thriftily
(Wel koude he dresse his takel yemanly:
His arwes drouped noght with fetheres lowe),
And in his hand he baar a mightly bowe.   90
A not heed [28] hadde he, with a broun visage.
Of wodecraft wel koude[29] he al the usage.
Upon his arm he baar a gay bracer,
And by his syde a swerd and a bokeler,
And on that oother syde a gay daggere   95
Harneised[30] wel and sharp as point of spere;
A Cristopher on his brest of silver sheene.
An horn he bar, the bawdryk was of grene;
A forster was he, soothly, as I gesse.

   Ther was also a NONNE, a PRIORESSE,   100
That of hir smylyng was ful symple and coy;
Hire gretteste ooth was but by Seinte Loy;
And she was cleped[31] madame Eglentyne.
Ful weel she soong the service dyvyne,
Entuned in hir nose ful semely,   105
And Frenssh she spak ful faire and fetisly,[32]
After the scole of Stratford atte Bowe,

---

22. coarse cloth   28. crew cut
23. doublet   29. knew
24. stained with his armor   30. equipped
25. hairs curled   31. named
26. yeoman   32. elegantly
 27. it pleased him to ride so

For Frenssh of Parys was to hire unknowe.
At mete wel ytaught was she with alle:
She leet no morsel from hir lippes falle, 110
Ne wette hir fyngres in hir sauce depe;
Wel koude she carie a morsel and wel kepe
That no drope ne fille upon hire brest.
In curtesie was set ful muchel hir lest.[33]
Hir over-lippe wyped she so clene 115
That in hir coppe ther was no ferthyng sene
Of grece, when she droken hadde hir draughte.
Ful semely after hir mete she raughte.[34]
And sikerly she was of greet desport,[35]
And ful pleasaunt, and amyable of port, 120
And peyned hire to countrefete cheere[36]
Of court, and to been estatlich[37] of manere,
And to ben holden digne of reverence.
But, for to speken of hire conscience,
She was so charitable and so pitous 125
She wolde wepe, if that she saugh a mous
Kaught in a trappe, if it were deed or bledde.
Of smale houndes hadde she that she fedde
With rosted flessh, or milk and wastel-breed.[38]
But soore wepte she if oon of hem were deed, 130
Of if men smoot it with a yerde smerte;
And al was conscience and tendre herte.

        *   *   *   *   *   *   *

   A MONK ther was, a fair for the maistrie,[39]
An outridere,[40] that loved venerie,[41]
A manly man, to been an abbot able. 140
Ful many a deyntee hors hadde he is stable,
And when he rood, men myghte his brydel heere
Gynglen in a whistlynge wynd als cleere
And eek as loude as dooth the chapel belle.
Ther as[42] this lord was kepere of the celle, 145
The reule of seint Maure or of seint Beneit,
By cause that it was old and somdel streit[43]
This ilke Monk leet olde thynges pace,
And heeled after the newe world the space.
He yaf[44] nat of that text a pulled hen 150

---

33. desire
34. reached
35. good nature
36. manners
37. stately
38. cake

39. quite a man
40. monastic inspector
41. hunting
42. inasmuch as
43. strict
44. gave

That seith that hunters been nat hooly men,
Ne that a monk, when he is recchelees,[45]
Is likned til a fissh that is waterlees, —
This is to seyn, a monk out of his cloystre.
But thilke text heeld he nat worth an oystre;   155
And I seyde his opinioun was good.
What sholde he studie and make hymselven wood,[46]
Upon a book in cloystre alwey to poure,
Or swynken[47] with his handes, and laboure,
As Austyn bit? How shal the world be served?   160
Lat Austyn have his swynk to hym reserved!
Therfore he was a prikasour[48] aright:
Grehoundes he hadde as swift as fowel in flight;
Of prikyng and of huntyng for the hare
Was al his lust, for no cost wolde he spare.   165
I seigh[49] his sleves purfiled[50] at the hond
With grys,[51] and that the fyeste of a lond;
And, for to festne his hood under his chyn,
He hadde of gold ywroght a ful curious pyn;
A love-knotte in the gretter ende ther was.   170
His heed was balled, that shoon as any glas,
And eek his face, as he hadde been enoynt.[52]
Te was a lord ful fat and in good poynt;[53]
His eyen stepe,[54] and rollynge in his heed,
That stemed as a forneys of a leed;[55]   175
His bootes souple, his hors in greet estaat.
Now certeinly he was a fair prelaat;
He was nat pale as a forpyned[56] goost.
A fat swan loved he best of any roost.
His palfrey was as broun as is a berye.   180

    A FRERE ther was, a wantowne and a merye,
A lymytour,[57] a ful solempne[58] man.
In alle the ordres foure is noon that kan
So muchel of daliaunce and fair langage.
He hadde maad ful many a mariage   185
Of yonge wommen at his owene cost.

45.	cloisterless	52.	anointed
46.	crazy	53.	condition
47.	work	54.	bright
48.	horseman	55.	cauldron
49.	saw	56.	tormented
50.	lined	57.	licensed beggar
51.	fur	58.	festive

Unto his ordre he was a noble post.[59]
Ful wel biloved and famulier was he
With frankeleyns over al in his contree,
And eek with worthy wommen of the toun;   190
For he hadde power of confessioun,
And seyde hymself, moore than a curat,
For of his ordre he was licenciat.[60]
Ful swetely herde he confessioun,
And pleasaunt was his absolucioun: 200
He was an esy man to yeve[61] penaunce,
Ther as he wiste to have a good pitaunce.
For unto a povre ordre for to yive
Is signe that a man is wel yshryve;
For if he yaf, he dorste make avaunt,[62]   205
He wiste that a man was repentaunt;
For many a man so hard is of his herte,
He may nat wepe, althogh hym soore smerte.
Therefore in stede of wepynge and preyeres
Men moote[63] yeve silver to the povre freres.   210
His typet was ay farsed[64] ful of knyves
And pynees, for to yeven faire wyves.
And certeinly he hadde a murye note:
Wel koude he synge and pleyen on a rote;[65]
Of yeddynges[66] he baar outrely the pris.   255
His nekke whit was as the flour-de-lys;
Therto he strong was as a champioun.
He knew the tavernes wel in every toun
And everich hostiler and tappestere
Bet[67] than a lazar or a beggestere;[68]   220
For unto swich a worthy man as he
Accorded nat, as by his facultee,
To have with sike lazars aqueyntaunce.
It is nat honest, it may nat avaunce,
For to deelen with no swich poraille,[69]   225
But al with riche and selleres of vitaille.
And over al, ther as profit sholde arise,
Curteis he was and lowely of servyse.
Ther nas no man nowher so vertuous.[70]
He was the beste beggere in his hous;   230

59. pillar
60. licensed to hear confessions anywhere
61. give
62. he dared to boast
63. should
64. stuffed
65. fiddle
66. songs
67. better
68. a leper or a beggar
69. trashy people
70. able

For thogh a wydwe hadde noght a sho,[71]
So plesaunt was his *"In principio,"*
Yet wolde he have a ferthyng, er he wente.
His purchas was wel bettre than his rente.
And rage[72] he koude, as it were right a whelp.   235
In love-dayes[73] ther koude he muchel help,
For ther he was nat lyk a cloysterer
With a thredbare cope, as is a povre scoler,
But he was lyk a maister or a pope.
Of double worstede was his semycope,   240
That rounded as a belle out of the presse.[74]
Somwhat he lipsed, for his wantownesse,
To make his Englissh sweete upon his tonge;
And in his harpyng, when that he hadde songe,
His eyen twynkled in his heed aryght,   245
As doon the sterres in the frosty nyght.
This worthy lymytour was cleped Huberd.

　　　*　　*　　*　　*　　*　　*　　*　　*

A CLERK ther was of Oxenford also,
That unto logyk hadde longe ygo.[75]
As leene was his hors as is a rake,   250
And he nas nat right fat, I undertake,
But looked holwe, and therto sobrely.
Ful thredbare was his overeste courtepy;[76]
For he hadde goten hym yet no benefice,
Ne was so wordly for to have office.[77]   255
For hym was levere[78] have at his beddes heed
Twenty bookes, clad in blak or reed,
Or Aristotle and his philosophie,
Than robes riche, or fithele,[79] or gay sautrie.
But al be that he was a philosophre,   260
Yet hadde he but litel gold in cofre;
But al that he myghte of his freendes hente,[81]
On bookes and on lernynge he it spente,
And bisiliy gan for the soules preye
Of hem that yaf hym wherwith to scoleye.[82]   265

---

71. shoe
72. romp
73. days for settling minor disputes
74. clothes press
75. gone
76. short coat

77. secular employment
78. he preferred
79. fiddle
80. psaltery
81. get
82. go to school

Of studie took he moost cure[83] and moost heede.
Noght o word spak he moore than was neede,
And that was seyd in forme and reverence,
And short and quyk and ful of hy sentence;[84]
Sownynge[85] in moral vertu was his speche,   270
And gladly wolde he lerne and gladly teche.

     *   *   *   *   *   *   *   *

     A good WIF was ther of biside BATHE,
But she was somdel deef, and that was scathe.[86]
Of clooth-makyng she hadde swich an haunt,[87]
She passed hem of Ypres and of Gaunt.   275
In al the parisshe wif ne was ther noon
That to the offrynge bifore hire sholde goon;
And if ther dide, certeyn so wrooth was she,
That she was out of alle charitee.
Hir coverchiefs ful fyne weren of ground;[88]   280
I dorste swere they weyeden ten pound
That on a Sonday weren upon hir heed.
Hir hosen weren of fyn scarlet reed,
Ful streite yteyd, and shoes ful moyste and newe.
Boold was hir face, and fair, and reed of hewe.   285
She was a worthy womman al hir lyve:
Housbondes at chirche dore she hadde fyve,
Withouten[89] oother campaigny in youthe, —
But therof nedeth nat to speke as nowthe.[90]
And thries hadde she been at Jerusalem;   290
She hadde passed many a straunge strem;
At Rome she hadde been, and at Boloigne,
In Galice at Seint Jame, and at Coloigne.
She koude muchel of wandrynge by the weye.
Gat-tothed[91] was she, soothly for to seye.   295
Upon an amblere esily she sat,
Ywympled wel, and on hir heed an hat
As brood as is a bokeler or a targe;
A foot-mantel aboute hir hipes large,
And on hir feet a paire of spores sharpe.
In felaweshipe wel koude she laughe and carpe.[92]   300

---

83.   care
84.   lofty ideas
85.   abounding
86.   a pity
87.   skill

88.   texture
89.   not to mention
90.   just now
91.   with teeth set wide apart
92.   talk

Of remedies of love she knew per chaunce,
For she koude of that art the olde daunce.[93]

A good man was ther of religioun,
And was a povre PERSOUN of a TOUN,   305
But riche he was of hooly thoght and werk.
He was also a lerned man, a clerk,
That Cristes gospel trewely wolde preche;
His parisshens devoutly wolde he teche.
Benygne he was, and wonder diligent,   310
And in adversitee ful pacient,
And swich he was ypreved ofte sithes.[94]
Ful looth were hym to cursen for his tithes,
But rather wolds he yeven, out of doute,
Unto his povre parisshens aboute   315
Of his offryng and eek of his substaunce.
He koude in litel thyng have suffisaunce.
Wyd was his parisshe, and houses fer asonder,
But he ne lefte nat, for reyn ne thonder,
In siknesse nor in meschief[95] to visite   320
The ferreste in his parisshe, muche and lite,[96]
Upon his feet, and in his hand a staf.
This noble ensample to his sheep he yaf,
That first he wroghte, and afterward he taughte.
Out of the gospel he tho wordes caughte,   325
And this figure he added eek therto,
That if gold ruste, what shal iren do?
For if a preest be foul, on whom we truste,
No wonder is a lewed[97] man to ruste;
And shame it is, if a prest take keep, [98]   330
A shiten shepherde and a clene sheep.
Wel oghte a preest ensample for to yive,
By his clennesse, how that his sheep sholde lyve.
He sette nat his benefice to hyre
And leet[99] his sheep encombred in the myre   335
And ran to Londoun unto Seinte Poules
To seken hym a chaunterie for soules,
Or with a bretherhed to been withholde;[100]
But dwelte at hoom, and kepte wel his folde,
So that the wold ne made in nat myscarie;   340

93.   she knew all the tricks of that art   **97. lay**
94.   times   98. heed
95.   misfortune   99. left
96.   of high and low estate   100. to be chaplain for a guild

He was a shepherde and noght a mercenarie.
And though he hooly were and vertuous,
He was to synful men nat despitous,
Ne of his speche daungerous[101] ne digne, [102]
But in his techyng discreet and benygne.   345
To drawen folk to hevene by fairnesse,
By good ensample, this was his bisynesse.
But it were any persone obstinat,
What so he were, of heigh or lough estat,
Hym wolde he snybben [103] sharply for the nonys.   350
A bettre preest I trowe that nowher noon ys.
He waited after no pompe and reverence,
Ne maked him a spiced conscience,
But Cristes loore and his apostles twelve
He taughte, but first he folwed it hymselve.   355

*   *   *   *   *   *   *   *

The MILLERE was a stout carl for the nones;
Ful byg he was of brawn, and eek of bones.
That proved wel,[104] for over al ther he cam,[105]
At wrastlynge he wolde have alwey the ram.
He was short-sholdred, brood, a thikke knarre;[106]   360
Ther was no dore that he nolde heve of harre,[107]
Or breke it and at rennyng with his heed.
His berd as any sowe or fox was reed,
And thereto brood, as though it were a spade.
Upon the cop[108] right of his nose he hade   365
A werte, and theron stood a toft of herys
Reed as the brustles of a sowes erys;
His nosethirles[109] blake were and wyde.
A swerd and bokeler bar he by his syde.
His mouth as greet was as a greet forneys.   370
He was a janglere[110] and a goliardeys, [111]
And that was moost of synne and harlotries.
Wel koude he stelen corn and tollen thries;
And yet he hadde a thombe of gold, pardee.
A whit coate and a blew hood wered he.   375
A baggepipe wel koude he blowe and sowne,[112]
And therwithal he broghte us out of towne.

---

101. overbearing   107. hinge
102. haughty   108. tip
103. rebuke   109. nostrils
104. was easily proved   110. idle talker
105. wherever he went   111. teller of dirty jokes
106. well-muscled fellow   112. sound

THE MILLERES TALE

[John, an elderly carpenter, married the beautiful Alisoun, very much his junior. The young bride attracted the attention of both Nicholas, an Oxford student boarding with the carpenter, and Absolon, the parish clerk. To get the husband out of the way in order that he may enjoy the bride, Nicholas persuades John that through his studies he has learned that a flood like Noah's is due; John, Alisoun, and Nicholas can be saved only if each spends the night suspended in a large tub high up near the ciling. There they are to pray vigorously, and the next day the waters will recede.

John obtains three tubs, and in the darkness all three climb up into them. When deep snores inform Nicholas and Alison that John is asleep, they climb down and leap happily into bed.

Meanwhile Absolon, not having seen the carpenter for some time, assumes that he is away, and that the present time, in the darkness, would be just right for him to display his charms to the fair Alisoun.]

When that the firste cok hath crowe, anoon
Up ryst this jolyf lover Absolon,
And him arrayeth gay, at poynt devys.[113]
But first he cheweth greyn and lycoris,
To smellen swete, or[114] he hadde kempt his heere.   5
Under his tunge a trewe love he beere,
For therby wende he to be gracious.
He rometh to the carpenteres hous,
And stille he stant under the schot wyndowe;
Unto his brest it raught, it was so lowe;   10
And softe he cowhith[115] with a semysoun:[116]
"What do ye, honycomb, swete Alisoun?
My faryre byrd, my swete cynamome,
Awake, lemman[117] myn, and speketh to me.
Ful litcl thynke ye upon my wo,   15
That for youre love I swelte[118] ther I go.
No wonder is if that I swelte and swete,
I morne as doth a lamb after the tete.[119]
I-wis, lemman, I have such love-longyng
That like a turtil trewe in my moornyng,   20
I may not ete no more than a mayde."

113. perfectly correct
114. before
115. cooes
116. half a sound
117. sweetheart
118. sweat
119. teat

"Go fro the wyndow, jakke fool," sche sayde,
"As help me God, it wol not be, compaine.[120]
I love another, and elles were I to blame,
Well bet than the, by Jhesu, Absolon.   25
Go forth thy wey, or I wol cast a stoon;
And let me slepe, a twenty devel way!"

"Allas!" quod Absolon, "and weylaway!
That trewe love was ever so ylle bysett;
Thanne kisseth me, syn it may be no bett,   30
For Jesus love, and for the love of me."

"Wilt thou then go thy wey therwith?" quod sche.

"Ye, certes, lemman," quod this Absolon.

"Then mak ye redy," quod sche, "I come anon."

This Absolon doun sette him on his knees,   35
And seide, "I am a lord at alle degrees;
For after this I hope ther cometh more;
Lemman, thy grace, and, swete byrd, thyn ore."[121]
The wyndow she undyd, and that in hast;
"Have doon," quod sche, "com of, and speed the fast, 40
Lest that our neygheboures the aspye."

This Absolon gan wipe his mouth ful drye,
Derk was the night as picche or as a cole,
Out atte wyndow putte sche hir hole:
And Absolon him fel no bet ne wers,   45
But with his mouth he kist hir naked ers
Ful savorly. When he was war of this,
Abak he sterte, and thought it was amys,
For wel he wist a womman hath no berd.
He felt a thing al rough and long y-herd,[122]   50
And seyde, "Fy, allas! what have I do?"

"Te-hee!" quod sche, and clapte the wyndow to;
And Absolon goth forth a sory paas.[123]

"A berd, a berd!" quod heende[124] Nicholas;
"By Goddes corps, this game goth fair and wel."   55

---

120. lovers
121. lips
122. haired

123. pace
124. handy

This seely Absolon herd every del,
And on his lippe he gan for angir byte;
And to himself he seyde, "I schal the quyte."

Who rubbith now, who froteth now his lippes
With dust, with sand, with straw, with cloth, with chippes, 60
But Absalon? that seith ful ofte. "Allas,
My soule bytake I unto Sathanas!125
But me were lever than alle this toun," quod he,
"Of this disprit awroken126 for to be.
Allas!" quod he, "allas! I nadde y-bleynt!127   65
His hoote love was cold, and al y-queint.
For fro that tyme that he hadde kist her ers,
Of paramours ne sette he nat a kers,
For he was helyd of his maledye;
Ful ofte paramours he gan deffyre,   70
And wept as doth a child that is y-bete.
A softe paas went he over the strete
Unto a smyth, men clepith daun128 Gerveys,
That in his forge smythcde plowh-harneys;
He scharpeth schar129 and culture130 bysily.   75
This Absolon knokketh all esily.
And seyde, "Undo, Gerveys, and that anoon."

"What, who art thou?"

"It am I Absolon."

"What? Absolon, what for Cristes swete tree!
Why ryse ye so rathe?131 *benedicite,*   80
What eyleth you? some gay gurl, God it woot,
Hath brought you thus upon the verytrot;
By seinte Noet! ye wote wel what I mene."
This Absolon ne wroughte nat a bene
Of all this play, no word agayn he yaf;   85
For he hadde more tow on his distaf
Than Gerveys knew, and seyde, "Freend so deere,
That hote cultre in the chymney heere
As lene132 it me, I have therwith to doone;
I wol it bring agayn to the ful soone."   90

---

125. Satan
126. avenged
127. blinded
128. sir

129. plowshare
130. harrow blade
131. early
132. lend

Gerveys answerde, "Certes, were it gold,
Or in a poke nobles all untold,
Ye schul him have, as I am trewe smyth.
Ey, Cristes fote! what wil ye do therwith?"

"Therof," quod Absolon, "be as be may;   95
I schal wel telle it the to morwe day";
And caughte the cultre by the colde stele,
Ful soft out at the dore he gan it stele,
And wente unto the carpenteres wal.
He cowheth first, and knokketh therwithal   100
Upon the wyndow, right as he dede er.[133]

This Alisoun answerde, "Who is ther
That knokketh so? I warant it a theef."

"Why nay," quod he, "God woot, my swete leef,
I am thyn Absolon, O my derlyng.   105
Of gold," quod he, "I have the brought a ryng;
My mooder yaf it me, so God me save!
Ful fyn it is, and therto wel y-grave;
This wol I yive the, if thou me kisse."

This Nicholas was risen for to pysse,   110
And thought he wold amenden[134] al the jape,[135]
He schulde kisse his ers or that[136] he skape.
And up the wyndow dyde he hastily,
And out his ers putteth he pryvely
Over the buttok, to the haunche bon.   115

And therwith spak this clerk, this Absolon,
"Spek, swete byrd, I wot nat wher thou art."

This Nicholas anon let flee a fart
As gret as it hadde ben a thundir dent,
And with that strook he was almost y-blent: 120
And he was redy with his yren hoot,
And Nicholas amid the ers he smoot.

Of[137] goth the skyn an hande brede[138] aboute.
The hoote cultre brente so his toute;

---

133. before
134. improve
135. trick

136. before
137. off
138. breadth

And for the smert he wende for to dye;   125
As he were wood,[139] anon he gan to crye,
"Help, watir, watir, help, for Goddes herte!"

     This carpentir out of his slumber sterte,
And herd on crye watir, as he wer wood.
He thought, "Allas, for now cometh Noes flood!"   130
He sit him up withoute wordes mo,
And with his ax he smot the corde a-two;
And doun he goth; he fond nowthir to selle
No breed ne ale, til he com to the selle
Upon the floor, and ther aswoun he lay.   135

     Up styrt hir Alisoun, and Nicholay,
And cryden, "Out and harrow!" in the strete,
The neygheboures bothe smal and grete
In ronnen, for to gauren[140] on this man,
That yet aswowne lay, bothe pale and wan;   140
For with the fal he brosten had his arm.
But stond he muste to his owne harm,
For when he spak, he was anon born doun
With heende Nicholas and Alisoun.
They tolden every man that he was wood;   145
 Hewas agast and feerd of Noes flood
Thurgh fantasye, that of his vanité
He hadde y-bought him knedying tubbes thre,
And hadde hem hanged in the roof above;
And that he preyed hem for Goddes love   150
To sitten in the roof par compaignye.[141]
The folk gan lawhen at his fantasye;
Into the roof they kyken, and they gape,
And torne al his harm into a jape.
For whatsoever the carpenter answerde,   155
Hit was for nought, no man his resoun herde,
With othes greet he was so sworn adoun,
That he was holden wood in all the toun.
For every clerk anon right heeld with othir;
They seyde, "The man was wood, my leeve brother";   160
And every man gan lawhen at his stryf.

---

139. crazy
140. stare
141. for company

Thus swyed was the carpenteres wyf
For al his kepyng and his gelousye;
And Absolon hath kist hir nether ye;
And Nicholas is skaldid in his towte.   165
This tale is doon, and God save al the route.

THE ELIZABETHEN ERA

After the death of Chaucer there were no major English poets for 150 years. While this lapse is puzzling, external events may explain it, at least in part. The first half of the fifteenth century was a time of conflict with France—the disastrous finale to the Hundred Years War. This period blended into that most confusing time of domestic troubles, the Wars of the Roses. In 1485 a competent (though hardly lovable) monarch, Henry VII, restored a certain stability, but his new Tudor dynasty was shortly confronted with the Reformation. His son, Henry VIII, for all his tempestuous ways, maneuvered Britain through this period with less bloodshed than might have been expected; even the sharp Protestant/Catholic/Protestant changes of direction under Edward VI, Mary, and Elizabeth were accompanied with comparatively modest blood-letting. Still, such times of turmoil do not lend themselves to the creation of poetry.

Poetry was of course being written. It must not be forgotten that the fifteenth century was the great time for the ballads; and one should also remember that the literary art in which the British have perhaps been most eminent—the drama—flourished in various forms from before the time of Chaucer all through the period in question.

While the reign of the first Elizabeth was not exactly a placid period, it did mark a return to a certain domestic stability. If "good Queen Bess" was a despot—and by our standards she certainly was—she was a most capable one, and she had the ability to choose capable subordinates. Furthermore, her unmarried status in a curious way seemed to suggest that her spouse was England—and in her reign the nationalism which her father and grandfather had fostered to strengthen their new dynasty reached extraordinary heights.

It was a proud time to be English. Military audacity eventually resulted in the defeat of the great Armada (1588); daring exploration brought in treasure and the beginnings of empire. The soldiers and sailors had their counterparts in artists. For literature in particular this was a golden age.

Although (or perhaps because) literature in English was in decline between Chaucer and Spenser, the language continued to evolve: Elizabethan English is very different from Middle English. It is in fact *Modern English*. There are occasional words and phrases in Shakespeare or the *Book of Common Prayer* which mystify us, but only occasional ones: people go happily to Shakespeare's plays and pray in Elizabethan English.

The most impressive Elizabethan literary achievement was the drama. Nearly all the plays were written at least partly in verse, and many entirely so—but the practical limits of space suggest that drama be treated elsewhere. We would do well to remember, however, that Elizabethan plays were popular entertainment. Admission prices were low, and ordinary folk paid them. Very possibly even ancient Athens did not expose more people to great literature than did Elizabethan England.

Outside the drama, the most notable form of Elizabethan poetry was the *sonnet*. Elizabethan writers used the *English sonnet* (iambic pentameter, 14 lines, three quatrains and a couplet, abab, cdcd, efef, gg), sometimes called *Shakespearean* (he wrote 154 of them), though the form is earlier than he.

Sonnets drew a different audience than plays. They are hard to write and so concentrated that they are often hard to understand. That they were written by the hundreds, often in long sequences, by highly learned men for the delight of one another tells us that English had "arrived" as a literary language. In fact the sonnet writers so reveled in English that they frequently played extravagant games with it: their poems abound in elaborate figures of speech. At their greatest these poems have the quality of exquisitely wrought jewelry; lesser poems suggest pleasant but not terribly important intellectual games.

The only major Elizabethan poet who did not also write plays was the earliest important figure of the period, Edmund Spenser (c.1552-1599). His masterpiece, *The Faerie Queene,* does not appeal to the modern reader, but in some respects it is typically Elizabethan. It is highly patriotic; it is an elaborate allegory, where each character stands for a person and usually a quality as well;[1] the language is yet more elaborated in that it is deliberately archaic. There are six Books to the poem; the first is well over 5000 lines long. Not surprisingly, therefore, readers enjoy certain individual scenes of splendor more than the entire complex work.

Spenser invented a special type of stanza for *The Faerie Queene;* called the *Spenserian stanza,* it is well suited to narrative and descriptive poetry, and has been used by many later poets. It contains eight lines of

---

1. The Faerie Queene herself, called Gloriana in the poem, is of course Elizabeth.

iambic pentameter and one of hexameter (called an *alexandrine*); the rhyme is ababbcbcc.

The most important Elizabethan poets are Shakespeare, Marlowe, and Jonson. Shakespeare needs no introduction; Marlowe *(Edward II, Doctor Faustus)* ranks high for the power of his verse and the depth of his penetration into human nature; Jonson *(Volpone)* has the humor lacking in Marlowe but lacks the breadth and depth. Shakespeare has many reasons for his fame, but perhaps the chief one is his mastery of all moods, from the subline to the delightfully ridiculous.

EDMUND SPENSER (c. 1552-1599)

FROM

THE FAERIE QUEENE, FIRST BOOK, CANTO I

1

A gentle Knight was pricking on the plaine,[1]
Ycladd in mightie armes and silver shielde,
Wherein old dints of deepe woundes did remaine,
The cruell markes of many a bloody fielde;
Yet armes till that time did he never wield.   5
His angry steede did chide his foming bitt,
As much disdayning to the curbe to yield:
Full jolly[2] knight he seemd, and faire did sitt,
As one for knightly giusts and fierce encounters fitt.

2

And on his brest a bloodie Crosse he bore,   10
The deare remembrance of his dying Lord,
For whose sweete sake that glorious badge he wore,
And dead, as living, ever him ador'd:
Upon his shield the like was also scor'd,
For soveraine hope which in his helpe he had.   15
Right faithfull true he was in deede and word,
But of his cheere did seeme too solemne sad;
Yet nothing did he dread, but ever was ydrad.[3]

3

Upon a great adventure he was bond,
The greatest Gloriana to him gave,   20
(That greatest Glorious Queene of Faery lond)
To winne him worshippe, and her grace to have,
Which of all earthly things he most did crave:
And ever as he rode his hart did earne[4]
To prove his puissance in battell brave   25
Upon his foe, and his new force to learne,
Upon his foe, a Dragon horrible and stearne.

---

1. Though Spenser's word ending superficially resemble Chaucer's, the reader will notice that the final *e* is no longer pronounced (though final *ed* is). Spenser's spelling is deliberately archaic.
2. handsome   4. yearn
3. dreaded

4

A lovelie Ladie rode him faire beside,
Upon a lowly Asse more white than snow,
Yet she much whiter; but the same did hide   30
Under a vele, that wimpled was full low;
And over all a blacke stole shee did throw:
As one that inly mournd, so was she sad,
And heavie sate upon her palfrey slow;
Seemed in heart some hidden care she had,   35
And by her, in a line, a milkewhite lambe she lad.

5

So pure and innocent, as that same lambe,
She was in life and every vertuous lore;
And by descent from Royall lynage came
Of ancient Kinges and Queenes, that had of yore   40
Their scepters stretcht from East to Westerne shore,
And all the world in their subjection held;
Till that infernall feend with foule uprore
Forewasted all their land, and them expeld;
Whom to avenge she had this Knight from far compeld.   45

TWO SONNETS FROM *AMORETTI*

30

My love is lyke to yse, and I to fyre;
Howe comes it then that this her cold so great
Is not dissolv'd through my so hot desyre,
But harder growes the more I her intreat?
Or how comes it that my exceeding heat   5
Is not delayd by her hart frosen cold,
But that I burne much more in boyling sweat,
And feele my flames augmented manifold?
What more miraculous thing may be told,
That fyre, which all things melts, should harden yse,   10
And yse, which is congealed with sencelesse cold,
Should kindle fyre by wonderful devyce?
    Such is the powre of love in gentle mind,
    That it can alter all the course of kynd.

79

Men call you fayre, and you doe credit it,
For that your selfe ye dayly such doe see:
But the trew fayre, that is the gentle wit
And vertuous mind, is much more praysd of me.
For all the rest, how ever fayre it be,   5
Shall turne to nought and loose that glorious hew:
But onely that is permanent and free
From frayle corruption, that doth flesh ensew.
That is true beautie: that doth argue you
To be divine and born of heavenly seed: 10
Deriv'd from that fayre Spirit from whom all true
And perfect beauty did at first proceed.
    He onely fayre, and what he fayre hath made:
    All other fayre, lyke flowers, untymely fade.

MICHAEL DRAYTON (1563-1631)

ODE XII FROM *THE BALLAD OF AGINCOURT*

Fair stood the wind for France,
When we our sails advance;
Nor now to prove our chance
    Longer will tarry;
But putting to the main,   5
At Caux, the mouth of Seine,
With all his martial train
    Landed King Harry.[1]

And taking many a fort,
Furnished in warlike sort,   10
Marcheth towards Agincourt
    In happy hour;
Skirmishing, day by day,
With those that stopped his way,
Where the French general lay   15
    With all his power.

---

1. Henry V

Which, to his height of pride,
King Henry to deride,
His ransom to provide,
   To the King sending;   20
Which he neglects the while,
As from a nation vile,
Yet, with an angry smile,
   Their fall portending.

And turning to his men,   25
Quoth our brave Henry then:
"Though they to one be ten,
   Be not amazed!
Yet have we well begun;
Battles so bravely won   30
Have ever to the sun
   By Fame been raised!

"And for myself," quoth he,
"This my full rest[2] shall be:
England ne'er mourn for me,   35
   Nor more esteem me!
Victor I will remain,
Or on this earth lie slain;
Never shall she sustain
Loss to redeem me!   40

"Poitiers and Cressy tell,
When most their pride did swell,
Under our swords they fell.
   No less our skill is,
Than when our grandsire great   45
Claiming the regal seat,
By many a warlike feat
   Lopped the French lilies."

The Duke of York so dread
The eager vanward led;   50
With the main, Henry sped
   Amongst his henchmen.
Exeter had the rear,
A braver man not there!
O Lord, how hot they were   55
   On the false Frenchmen!

---

2. decision

They now to fight are gone,
Armor on armor shone,
Drum now to drum did groan;
   To hear, was wonder;   60
That, with the cries they make,
The very earth did shake;
Trumpet to trumpet spake;
   Thunder to thunder.

Well it thine age became,   65
O noble Erpingham,
Which did the signal aim
   To our hid forces!
When from a meadow by,
Like a storm suddenly,   70
The English archery
   Struck the French horses.

With Spanish yew so strong,
Arrows a cloth-yard long,
That like to serpents stung,   75
   Piercing the weather.
None from his fellow starts;
But, playing the manly parts,
And like true English hearts,
   Stuck close together.   80

When down their bows they threw,
And forth their bilboes[3] drew,
And on the French they flew:
   Not one was tardy.
Arms were from shoulders sent,   85
Scalps to the teeth were rent,
Down the French peasants went;
   Our men were hardy.

This while our noble King,
His broad sword brandishing,   90
Down the French host did ding,[4]
   As to o'erwhelm it;
And many a deep wound lent,
His arms with blood besprent,
And many a cruel dent   95
   Bruised his helmet.

---

3.   swords   4.   strike

Gloucester, that duke so good,
Next of the royal blood,
For famous England stood,
    With his brave brother.   100
Clarence, in steel so bright,
Though but a maiden knight,
Yet in that furious fight,
    Scarce such another!

Warwick in blood did wade,   105
Oxford, the foe invade,
And cruel slaughter made,
    Still as they ran up.
Suffolk his axe did ply;
Beaumont and Willoughby,   110
Bear them right doughtily,
    Ferrers, and Fanhope.

Upon Saint Crispin's Day[5]
Fought we this noble Fray;
Which Fame did not delay   115
    To England to carry.
O when shall English men
With such acts fill a pen?
Or England breed again
    Such a King Harry?   120

CHRISTOPHER MARLOWE (1564-1593)

HELEN (FROM *DOCTOR FAUSTUS*)

Was this the face that launched a thousand ships,
And burned the topless towers of Ilium? —
Sweet Helen, make me immortal with a kiss! —
Her lips suck forth my soul: see where it flees! —
Come, Helen, come, give me my soul again.   5
Here will I dwell, for heaven is in these lips,
And all is dross that is not Helena.
I will be Paris, and for love of thee,

---

5.   October 25, 1415

Instead of Troy, shall Wittenberg[1] be sacked,
And I will combat with weak Menelaus,   10
And wear thy colors on my plumed crest;
Yes, I will wound Achilles in the heel,
And then return to Helen for a kiss.
Oh, thou art fairer than the evening air
Clad in the beauty of a thousand stars;   15
Brighter art thou than flaming Jupiter
When he appeared to hapless Semele;
More lovely than the monarch of the sky
In wanton Arethusa's azured arms;
And none but thou shall be my paramour!   20

"WHO EVER LOVED, THAT LOVED NOT AT FIRST SIGHT?"

It lies not in our power to love or hate,
For will in us is overruled by fate.
When two are stripped,[2] long ere the course begin,
We wish that one should lose, the other win;
And one especially do we affect   5
Of two gold ingots, like in each respect:
The reason no man knows; let it suffice
What we behold is censured by our eyes.
Where both deliberate, the love is slight:
Who ever loved, that loved not at first sight?   10

THE PASSIONATE SHEPHERD TO HIS LOVE

Come live with me, and be my love;
And we will all the pleasures prove
That hills and valleys, dales and fields,
Woods, or steepy mountain yields.

And we will sit upon the rocks,   5
Seeing the shepherds feed their flocks
By shallow rivers, to whose falls
Melodious birds sing madrigals.

And I will make thee beds of roses,
And a thousand fragrant posies;   10
A cap of flowers, and a kirtle[3]
Embroidered all with leaves of myrtle;

---

1. The home of Faustus, who is speaking   3. gown or skirt
2. Stripped down for a course, or race

A gown made of the finest wool
Which from our pretty lambs we pull;
Fair-lined slippers for the cold,   15
With buckles of the purest gold;

A belt of straw and ivy-buds,
With coral clasps and amber studs;
And if these pleasures may thee move,
Come live with me, and be my love.   20

The shepherd-swains shall dance and sing
For thy delight each May morning;
If these delights thy mind may move,
Then live with me, and be my love.

WILLIAM SHAKESPEARE (1564-1616)

SONGS FROM THE PLAYS

From *Love's Labor's Lost*

When icicles hang by the wall,
    And Dick the shepherd blows his nail,
And Tom bears logs into the hall,
    And milk comes frozen home in pail,
When blood is nipped and ways be foul,   5
Then nightly sings the staring owl,
"To-whit, Tu-whoo!" A merry note,
While greasy Joan doth keel[1] the pot.

When all about the wind doth blow,
    And coughing drowns the parson's saw,   10
And birds sit brooding in the snow,
    And Marian's nose looks red and raw;
When roasted crabs hiss in the bowl —
Then nightly sings the staring owl,
"To-whit, Tu-whoo!" A merry note,   15
While greasy Joan doth keel the pot.

---

1. cool by stirring

From *Cymbeline*

Hark, hark! the lark at heaven's gate sings,
    And Phoebus 'gins arise,
His steeds to water at those springs
    On chaliced flowers that lies;
And winking Mary-buds begin   5
    To ope their golden eyes:
With every thing that pretty bin,
    My lady sweet, arise:
        Arise, arise!

*   *   *

Fear no more the heat o' th' sun,
    Nor the furious winter's rages;
Thou thy worldly task hast done,
    Home art gone, and ta'en thy wages:
Golden lads and girls all must,   5
As chimney sweepers, come to dust.

Fear no more the frown o' th' great;
    Thou art past the tyrant's stroke;
Care no more to clothe and eat;
    To thee the reed is as the oak: 10
The sceptre, learning, physic, must
All follow this, and come to dust.

Fear no more the lightning-flash,
    Nor th' all-dreaded thunder-stone;
Fear not slander, censure rash;   15
    Thou hast finished joy and moan:
All lovers young, all lovers must
Consign to thee, and come to dust.

No exorciser harm thee!
    Nor no witchcraft charm thee!   20
Ghost unlaid forbear thee!
    Nothing ill come near thee!
Quiet consummation have;
And renowned be thy grave!

From *Twelfth Night*

O Mistress mine, where are you roaming?
O stay and hear! your true-love's coming,
 That can sing both high and low;
Trip no further, pretty sweeting,
Journeys end in lovers meeting —   5
 Every wise man's son doth know.

What is love? 'tis not hereafter;
Present mirth hath present laughter;
 What's to come is still unsure:
In delay there lies no plenty, —   10
Then come kiss me, sweet-and-twenty,
 Youth's a stuff will not endure.

From *The Tempest*

Full fathom five thy father lies:
 Of his bones are coral made;
Those are pearls that were his eyes;
 Nothing of him that doth fade
But doth suffer a sea-change   5
Into something rich and strange.
Sea-nymphs hourly ring his knell:
 Hark! now I hear them, —
  Ding, dong, bell.

SONNETS

18

Shall I compare thee to a summer's day?
Thou are more lovely and more temperate:
Rough winds do shake the darling buds of May,
And summer's lease hath all too short a date:
Sometimes too hot the eye of heaven shines,   5
And often is his gold complexion dimmed;
And every fair² from fair sometime declines,
By chance, or nature's changing course untrimmed;
But thy eternal summer shall not fade,
Nor lose possession of that fair thou owest;   10
Nor shall Death brag thou wand'rest in his shade,
When in eternal lines to time thou growest:
 So long as men can breathe or eyes can see,
 So long lives this, and this gives life to thee.

---

2. beauty

29

When, in disgrace with fortune and men's eyes,
I all alone beweep my outcast state,
And trouble deaf heaven with my bootless cries,
And look upon myself and curse my fate,
Wishing me like to one more rich in hope,   5
Featured like him, like him with friends possessed,
Desiring this man's art and that man's scope,
With what I most enjoy contented least;
Yet in these thoughts myself almost despising,
Haply I think on thee, — and then my state,   10
Like to the lark at break of day arising
From sullen earth, sings hymns at heaven's gate;
    For thy sweet love remembered such wealth brings
    That then I scorn to change my state with kings.

33

Full many a glorious morning have I seen
Flatter the mountain-tops with sovereign eye,
Kissing with golden face the meadows green,
Gilding pale streams with heavenly alchemy:
Anon permit the basest clouds to ride   5
With ugly rack on his celestial face,
And from the forlorn world his visage hide,
Stealing unseen to west with his disgrace:
Even so my sun one early morn did shine
With all-triumphant splendor on my brow;   10
But out! alack! he was but one hour mine;
The region cloud hath masked him from me now.
    Yet him for this my love no whit disdaineth;
    Suns of the world may stain[3] when heaven's sun staineth.

---

3. become darkened

73

That time of year thou mayst in me behold
When yellow leaves, or none, or few, do hang
Upon those boughs which shake against the cold,
Bare ruined choirs, where late the sweet birds sang.
In me thou see'st the twilight of such day   5
As after sunset fadeth in the west,
Which by and by black night doth take away,
Death's second self, that seals up all in rest.
In me thou see'st the glowing of such fire
That on the ashes of his youth doth lie,   10
As the death-bed whereon it must expire,
Consumed with that which it was nourished by.
   This thou perceivest, which makes thy love more strong,
   To love that well which thou must leave ere long.

116

Let me not to the marriage of true minds
Admit impediments. Love is not love
Which alters when it alteration finds,
Or bends with the remover to remove:
O, no! it is an ever-fixèd mark   5
That looks on tempests and is never shaken;
It is the star to every wandering bark,
Whose worth's unknown, although his height be taken.
Love's not Time's fool, though rosy lips and cheeks
Within his bending sickle's compass come;   10
Love alters not with his brief hours and weeks,
But bears it out even to the edge of doom.
   If this be error and upon me proved,
   I never writ, nor no man ever loved.

130

My mistress' eyes are nothing like the sun;
Coral is far more red than her lips' red;
If snow be white, why then her breasts are dun;
If hairs be **wires, black wires** grow on her head.
I have seen roses damasked, red and white,   5
But no such roses see I in her cheeks;
And in some perfumes is there more delight
Than in the breath that from my mistress reeks.
I love to hear her speak, yet well I know
That music hath a far more pleasing sound;   10
I grant I never saw a goddess go;
My mistress, when she walks, treads on the ground:
    And yet, by heaven, I think my love as rare
    As any she belied with false compare.

BEN JONSON (1573-1637)

SONG TO CELIA

Drink to me only with thine eyes,
    And I will pledge with mine;
Or leave a kiss but in the cup,
    And I'll not look for wine.
The thirst that from the soul doth rise   5
    Doth ask a drink divine;
But might I of Jove's nectar sup,
    I would not change for thine.

I sent thee late a rosy wreath
    Not so much honoring thee,   10
As giving it a hope that there
    It could not withered be.
But thou thereon didst only breathe,
    And sent'st it back to me;
Since when it grows, and smells, I swear,   15
    Not of itself, but thee.

TO THE MEMORY OF MY BELOVED MASTER, WILLIAM SHAKESPEARE

To draw no envy, Shakespeare, on thy name,
Am I thus ample to thy book and fame;
While I confess thy writings to be such
As neither man, nor muse, can praise too much.
'Tis true, and all men's suffrage. But these ways   5
Were not the paths I meant unto thy praise;
For silliest ignorance on these may light,
Which, when it sounds at best, but echoes right;
Or blind affection, which doth ne'er advance
The truth, but gropes, and urgeth all by chance;   10
Or crafty malice might pretend this praise,
And think to ruin, where it seemed to raise.
These are, as[1] some infamous bawd or whore
Should praise a matron. What could hurt her more?
But thou are proof against them, and, indeed,   15
Above the ill fortune of them, or the need.
I therefore will begin. Soul of the age!
The applause, delight, and wonder of our stage!
My Shakespeare, rise! I will not lodge thee by
Chaucer, or Spenser, or bid Beaumont lie   20
A little farther off, to make thee a room:
Thou art a monument without a tomb,
And art alive still while thy book doth live
And we have wits to read and praise to give.
That I not mix thee so, my brain excuses,   25
I mean with great, but disproportioned Muses;
For if I thought my judgment were of years,
I should commit thee surely with thy peers,
And tell how far thou didst our Lyly outshine,
Our sporting Kyd, or Marlowe's mighty line.   30
And though thou hadst small Latin and less Greek,
From thence to honor thee, I would not seek
For names; but call forth thundering Aeschylus,
Euripides, and Sophocles to us;
Pacuvius, Accius, him of Cordova[2] dead,   35
To life again, to hear thy buskin tread,
And shake a stage; or, when thy socks were on,

---
1. as if
2. Seneca

Leave thee alone for the comparison
Of all that insolent Greece or haughty Rome
Set forth, or since did from their ashes come.   40
Triumph, my Britain, thou hast one to show
To whom all scenes of Europe homage owe.
He was not of an age, but for all time!
And all the Muses still were in their prime,
When, like Apollo, he came forth to warm   45
Our ears, or like a Mercury to charm!
Nature herself was proud of his designs,
And joyed to wear the dressing of his lines!
Which were so richly spun, and woven so fit,
As, since, she will vouchsafe no other wit.   50
The merry Greek, tart Aristophanes,
Neat Terence, witty Plautus, now not please;
But antiquated and deserted lie,
As they were not of Nature's family.
Yet must I not give Nature all; thy art,   55
My gentle Shakespeare, must enjoy a part.
For though the poet's matter Nature be,
His art doth give the fashion; and, that he
Who casts to write a living line, must sweat,
(Such as thine are) and strike the second heat   60
Upon the Muses' anvil; turn the same
(And himself with it) that he thinks to frame,
Or, for the laurel, he may gain a scorn;
For a good poet's made, as well as born.
And such wert thou! Look how the father's face   65
Lives in his issue, even so the race
Of Shakespeare's mind and manners brightly shines
In his well turned, and true filed lines;
In each of which he seems to shake a lance,
As brandished at the eyes of ignorance.   70
Sweet Swan of Avon! what a sight it were
To see thee in our water yet appear,
And make those flights upon the banks of Thames
That so did take Eliza, and our James![3]
But stay, I se thee in the hemisphere   75
Advanced, and made a constellation there!
Shine forth, thou star of poets, and with rage
Of influence, chide or cheer the drooping stage,

---

3. James I

Which, since thy flight from hence, hath mourned like night,
And despairs day, but for thy volume's light.   80

> [These generous lines from a rival playwright
> were written for the First Folio of Shakes-
> peare's plays, published seven years after
> Shakespeare's death, in 1623.]

V

THE SEVENTEENTH CENTURY

It is the nature of the human mind to desire things to be tidy—neatly stacked into appropriate pigeon-holes. Literary history would be far simpler to study if at a given time, upon a given signal, all writers wrote differently from the way they had written before—and all changed in the same way. This natural desire to categorize must be followed to some extent if we are to avoid chaos, but the student should be aware of its limitations.

For example, seventeenth century Britain went through experiences very much unlike those of a century before, and hence it quite naturally wrote differently. Those differences will be noted. However, at any particular time a particular writer was not likely to think of himself as of any particular school, and many men who seem alike to us saw no resemblances between themselves—if indeed they were even aware of each other. The categories are almost always supplied by critics of a later era, and they should be taken as guides only, not as definitive divisions.

The period from 1600 through 1699 has no particular significance; the "seventeenth century" might more properly be considered to run from 1603 through 1688. These years were a time of almost continuous conflict within Britain, and it is perhaps this civil strife which best distinguishes the seventeenth century from the Elizabethan era.

There were actually at least three different kinds of conflict. One variety was *political:* it centered on the struggle for supremacy between King and Parliament. Although Elizabeth (as has been said) ruled without much concern for protecting opposing views, she was shrewd enough —and perhaps lucky enough—to get away with it. The four Stuart Kings —James I, Charles I, Charles II, and James II—were not. They felt (as doubtless did Elizabeth) that they ruled by divine right, but Parliament became increasingly harder to convince of this fact.[1] The conflict cost

---

1. The Stuarts were Scottish, and only Charles II really seemed to understand his English subjects. Elizabeth dying unmarried, it was arranged that her cousin, James of Scotland, would become James I of England and rule over both Kingdoms.

Charles I his head, and featured civil war and dictatorship under the "Lord Protector," Oliver Cromwell. In the end the struggle was won by Parliament. After the "Glorious Revolution" of 1688 disposed of James II, Parliament brought in his daughter, Mary, and her husband, the Dutch William of Orange. Parliament having created, Parliament could destroy, and no longer was there question about the ultimate source of power.

A second conflict was *religious*. Although the Stuarts had various Roman Catholic connections and inclinations, the issue was not really Roman Catholicism; rather it was the extent of the English Reformation. On the one hand stood the Church of England—no longer Roman but certainly still partly "catholic" (in its vestments, its liturgy, its ceremonial)—and on the other the more extreme reformers who felt that reform had not gone far enough. Though the reforming groups disagreed sharply among themselves, they generally adhered to the views of John Calvin and were given the name *Puritans*. For a while the Puritans prevailed, but in the end the Anglican Church was restored—with the understanding that increasing toleration would be given other Protestants (but not Catholics) to practice their faith in their own ways.

A third conflict was *economic*. It was less conspicuous than the others, but unquestionably it was important. In essence it involved the old landed interest on the one hand and the rising class of merchants on the other. That the dominant policy of the next century was "mercantilism" is sufficient proof of the eventual winner.

These conflicts cut across society in various ways. Typically the Royalists, Anglicans, and country squires were opposed to the Parliamentarians, Puritans, and merchants, but until war cut the country in half, it was possible for a Parliamentarian merchant to be a devout Anglican, and there were country squires with Puritan leanings who supported the King.

Certain generalizations can be made about what such a time means for poety. Because poety is primarily concerned with feeling, it is not too likely to flourish in an age of argument (though other arts do; the seventeenth century was perhaps the supreme age of the mathematician); and such poetry as is written is more likely to "talk" than to "sing." Furthermore, in an age of strife, particularly religious strife, men seek for the fundamentals, for truth; and while truth and beauty may be the same in the last analysis, they are reached in different ways, and poetry seeking truth is likely to be difficult and philosophical.

With the usual exceptions, these generalizations hold true for the seventeenth century. There was one great poet (Milton), who is above generalizations; most of the others are interesting, philosophical, and difficult. If the end of this last sentence suggests a kinship between the seventeenth century and our own, this is not surprising: we too live in an age of strife, and our poetry tends to be interesting, philosophical, and difficult.

The most typical seventeenth century poets have been classified (though not by themselves) as *metaphysical*. Their difficulty lies chiefly in their use of "conceits" — elaborate and usually extended metaphors where a parallel is drawn between quite unlike objects or situations. Metaphysical poetry also tends to be highly concentrated, and harsh in sound — all of which qualities make for difficult reading. On the other hand, the poets (in Dr. Johnson's words) "sometimes struck out unexpected truth."

The metaphysical poets, learned men writing highly intellectual poetry for a limited audience, chose profound subjects for their poems: God, love, death, time. The underlying seriousness was sometimes masked by a superficial levity, since the conceit by definition was concerned with the comparison of things unlike each other. The most important figure of this group was John Donne; other well known personages were George Herbert, Henry Vaughan, and Andrew Marvell.

Different from the metaphysical poets were the so-called *cavaliers*, or neo-classicists. They objected to the extravagances of Elizabethan and metaphysical poetry and aimed for the harmony and proportion that they thought of as "classic." Of all English writers they most admired Ben Jonson, and some called themselves "sons of Ben." Their style was to become dominant by the end of the century; in the period under study they were best represented by Robert Herrick.

Major figures usually transcend the limitations of their era, and hence John Milton fits into no pigeon-hole. Though a devout Puritan, he lacked the harshness and gracelessness that marred the Puritan personality. Before the Puritan revolution he wrote a number of lyrics of a general cavalier variety—graceful, artificial, full of classical learning. During the Civil War and Protectorate he became Latin Secretary to Cromwell's government (Marvell was his assistant) and almost literally gave his all to the cause; he did lose his sight. Most of his writing in this period was prose. Finally, after the Restoration, blind and obviously discouraged by the loss of all he had fought for, Milton dictated the three long blank verse poems on which his reputation primarily rests: *Paradise Lost, Paradise Regained,* and *Samson Agonistes* (Samson "the Struggler"). The first tells of the fall of man; the second of his redemption by Christ's resisting the temptations of Satan which Adam had succumbed to; the third (quite appropriately) of the Old Testament blind warrior in the enemy's hands.

Milton's epics are monumental in length as well as in scope: *Paradist Lost* runs for some 10,000 lines. In an age of abridgements and condensations it does not fare well; but even the reader who blanches at the thought of going straight through it must be impressed with the grandeur and sonority of the verse.

Since the seventeenth century was a time of religious concern and religious conflict, it is appropriate that its most important book by far was the *King James Bible* (1611). Neither the first nor the last English translation, this "noblest monument of English prose" continues to hold its own even in our time because of its mixture of simplicity, vigor, and splendor. James I did not translate it himself, but he was responsible for collecting the scholars who did, and the "Authorized Version" must be considered as one of the great achievements of a less-than-great reign.

The Bible is of course in prose, but much of the Hebrew and some of the Greek from which it was translated were not; and the cadences of the original verse frequently come through into the grand rhythms of the translation.

FROM THE KING JAMES BIBLE (1611)

WISDOM

But where shall wisdom be found?
    and where is the place of understanding?
Man knoweth not the price thereof;
    neither is it found in the land of the living.
The depth saith, "It is not in me":
    And the sea saith, "It is not with me."
It cannot be gotten for gold,
    neither shall silver be weighed for the price thereof.
It cannot be valued with the gold of Ophir,   5
    with the precious onyx, or the sapphire.
The gold and the crystal cannot equal it:
    and the exchange of it shall not be for jewels of fine gold.
No mention shall be made of coral, or of pearls:
    for the price of wisdom is above rubies.
The topaz of Ethiopia shall not equal it,
    neither shall it be valued with pure gold.
Whence then cometh wisdom?
    and where is the place of understanding?
Seeing it is hid from the eyes of all living,   10
    and kept close from the fowls of the air.
Destruction and death say,
    "We have heard the fame thereof with our ears."
God understandeth the way thereof,
    and he knoweth the place thereof.
For he looketh to the ends of the earth,
    and seeth under the whole heaven;
To make the weight for the winds;
    and he weigheth the waters by measure.
When he made a decree for the rain,   15
    and a way for the lightning of the thunder;
Then did he see it, and declare it;
    he prepared it, yea, and searched it out.
And unto man he said, "Behold, the fear of the Lord, that is wisdom;
    and to depart from evil is understanding."

                  Job, XXVIII, 12-28

PSALM XXIII

The Lord is my shepherd;
     I shall not want.
He maketh me to lie down in green pastures:
     He leadeth me beside the still waters.
He restoreth my soul:
     he leadth me in the paths of righteousness for his name's sake.
Yea, though I walk through the valley of the shadow of death,
     I will fear no evil:
          For thou art with me; thy rod and thy staff they comfort me.
Thou preparest a table before me in the presence of mine enemies: 5
     thou anointest my head with oil; my cup runneth over.
Surely goodness and mercy shall follow me all the days of my life:
     and I will dwell in the house of the Lord forever.

COMFORT

Comfort ye, comfort ye my people,
     saith your God.
Speak ye comfortably to Jerusalem, and cry unto her,
     that her warfare is accomplished, that her iniquity is pardoned:
          for she hath received of the Lord's hand
               double for all her sins.
The voice of him that crieth in the wilderness,
     "Prepare ye the way of the Lord,
          make straight in the desert a highway for our God.
"Every valley shall be exalted,
     and every mountain and hill shall be made low:
          and the crooked shall be made straight,
             and the rough places plain.
"And the glory of the Lord shall be revealed,   5
     and all flesh shall see it together:
          for the mouth of the Lord hath spoken it."
                            Isaiah, XL, 1-5

JOHN DONNE (1573-1631)

SONG

Go and catch a falling star,
    Get[1] with child a mandrake root,
Tell me where all times past are,
    Or who cleft the Devil's foot;
Teach me to hear mermaids singing,   5
Or·to keep off envy's stinging,
        And find
        What wind
Serves to advance an honest mind.

If thou be'st born to strange sights,   10
    Things invisible go see,
Ride ten thousand days and nights
    Till age snow white hairs on thee;
Thou, when thou return'st, wilt tell me
All strange wonders that befell thee,   15
        And swear
        No where
Lives a woman true and fair.

If thou find'st one let me know,
    Such a pilgrimage were sweet;   20
Yet do not, I would not go,
    Though at next door we might meet:
Though she were true when you met her,
And last till you write your letter,
        Yet she   25
        Will be
False, ere I come, to two or three.

THE GOOD-MORROW

I wonder, by my troth, what thou and I
Did, till we loved? were we not weaned till then?
But sucked on country pleasures, childishly?
Or snorted we in the Seven Sleepers' den?
'Twas so; but this, all pleasures fancies be;   5
If ever any beauty did I see,
Which I desired, and got, 'twas but a dream of thee.

---

1.   beget

And now good-morrow to our waking souls,
Which watch not one another out of fear;
For love all love of other sights controls,　　　　10
And makes one little room an everywhere.
Let sea-discoverers to new worlds have gone;
Let maps to other, worlds on worlds have shown;
Let us possess one world; each hath one, and is one.

My face in thine eye, thine in mine appears,　　　15
And true plain hearts do in the faces rest;
Where can we find two better hemispheres
Without sharp north, without declining west?
Whatever dies, was not mixed equally;
If our two loves be one, or thou and I　　　　　20
Love so alike that none can slacken, none can die.

THE SUN RISING

　Busy old fool, unruly Sun,
　　Why dost thou thus,
Through windows, and through curtains, call on us?
Must to thy motions lovers' seasons run?
　　Saucy pedantic wretch, go chide　　　　5
　　Late school-boys and sour prentices,
　Go tell court-huntsmen that the king will ride,
　Call country ants to harvest offices:
Love, all alike, no season knows nor clime,
Nor hours, days, months, which are the rags of time.　10

　Thy beams so reverend and strong
　　Why shouldst thou think?
I could eclipse and cloud them with a wink,
But that I would not lose her sight so long.
　　If her eyes have not blinded thine,　　　15
　　Look, and tomorrow late tell me,
　Whether both th' Indias of spice and mine
　Be where thou left'st them, or lie here with me.
Ask for those kings whom thou saw'st yesterday,
And thou shalt hear, "All here in one bed lay."　　20

She's all states, and all princes I:
  Nothing else is;
Princes do but play us; compared to this,
All honor's mimic, all wealth alchemy.
   Thou, Sun, art half as happy as we,   25
   In that the world's contracted thus;
  Thine age asks ease, and since thy duties be
  To warm the world, that's done in warming us.
Shine here to us, and thou art everywhere;
This bed thy centre is, these walls thy sphere.   30

"BATTER MY HEART"

Batter my heart, three-personed God; for you
As yet but knock, breathe, shine, and seek to mend.
That I may rise and stand, o'erthrow me and bend
Your force to break, blow, burn and make me new.
I, like an usurped town, to another due,   5
Labor to admit you, but, oh, to no end;
Reason, your viceroy in me, me should defend,
But is captived and proves weak or untrue.
Yet dearly I love you and would be loved fain,
But am bethrothed unto your enemy: 10
Divorce me, untie or break that knot again,
Take me to you, imprison me, for I,
Except you enthrall me, never shall be free,
Nor ever chaste, except you ravish me.

"DEATH, BE NOT PROUD"

Death, be not proud, though some have called thee
Mighty and dreadful, for thou art no so;
For those whom thou think'st thou dost overthrow
Die not, poor Death; nor yet canst thou kill me.
From Rest and Sleep, which but thy pictures be,   5
Much pleasure, then from thee much more must flow;
And soonest our best men with thee do go,
Rest of their bones and souls' delivery!
Thou art slave to fate, chance, kings, and desperate men,
And dost with poison, war, and sickness dwell;   10
And poppy or charms can make us sleep as well
And better than thy stroke. Why swell'st thou then?
One short sleep past, we wake eternally,
And Death shall be no more: Death, thou shalt die!

ROBERT HERRICK (1591-1674)

THE ARGUMENT OF HIS BOOK

I sing of brooks, of blossoms, birds, and bowers,
Of April, May, of June, and July flowers;
I sing of May-poles, hock-carts, wassails, wakes,
Of bridegrooms, brides, and of their bridal cakes.
I write of Youth, of Love, and have access   5
By these, to sing of cleanly wantonness;
I sing of dews, of rains, and, piece by piece,
Of balm, of oil, of spice, and ambergris;
I sing of times trans-shifting; and I write
How roses first came red, and lilies white;   10
I write of groves, of twilights, and I sing
The court of Mab, and of the Fairy King.
I write of Hell; I sing and ever shall,
O Heaven, and hope to have it after all.

TO THE VIRGINS, TO MAKE MUCH
OF TIME

Gather ye rosebuds while ye may,
    Old Time is still a-flying;
And this same flower that smiles today,
    To-morrow will be dying.

The glorious lamp of heaven, the sun,   5
    The higher he's a-getting,
The sooner will his race be run,
    And nearer he's to setting.

That age is best which is the first,
    When youth and blood are warmer;   10
But being spent, the worse, and worst
    Times, still succeed the former.

Then be not coy, but use your time,
    And while ye may, go marry;
For, having lost but once your prime,   15
    You may forever tarry.

THREE POEMS ON BEN JONSON

Fill me a mighty bowl
  Up to the brim;
  That I may drink
Unto my Jonson's soul.

Crown it again, again;   5
  And thrice repeat
  That happy heat,
To drink to thee, my Ben.

Well I can quaff, I see,
  To th' number five,   10
  Or nine, but thrive
In frenzy ne'er like thee.

*   *   *   *   *   *

When I a verse shall make,
  Know I have prayed thee,
For old religion's sake,
  Saint Ben, to aid me.

Make the way smooth for me,   5
  When I, thy Herrick,
Honoring thee, on my knee
  Offer my Lyric.

Candles I'll give to thee,
  And a new altar;   10
And thou, Saint Ben, shalt be
  Writ in my psalter.

*   *   *   *   *

Here lies Jonson with the rest
Of the poets, but the best.
Reader, wouldst thou more have known?
Ask his story, not this stone;
That will speak what this can't tell   5
Of his glory. So farewell.

DELIGHT IN DISORDER

A sweet disorder in the dress
Kindles in clothes a wantonness:
A lawn about the shoulders thrown
Into a fine distraction;
An erring lace, which here and there   5
Enthrals the crimson stomacher;
A cuff neglectful, and thereby
Ribbons to flow confusedly;
A winning wave, deserving note,
In the tempestuous petticoat;   10
A careless shoe-string, in whose tie
I see a wild civility;
Do more bewitch me, than when art
Is too percise in every part.

TO DAFFODILS

Fair daffodils, we weep to see
  You haste away so soon:
As yet the early-rising sun
  Has not attained his noon.
    Stay, stay,   5
  Until the hasting day
   Has run
  But to the even-song;
And, having prayed together, we
  Will go with you along.   10

We have short time to stay, as you,
  We have as short a Spring!
As quick a growth to meet decay
  As you, or any thing.
    We die,   15
  As your hours do, and dry
   Away,
  Like to the Summer's rain;
Or as the pearls of morning's dew
  Ne'er to be found again.   20

GEORGE HERBERT (1953-1633)

LOVE

Love bade me welcome; yet my soul drew back,
    Guilty of dust and sin.
But quick-eyed Love, observing me grow slack
    From my first entrance in,
Drew nearer to me, sweetly questioning,   5
    If I lacked anything.

"A guest," I answered, "worthy to be here";
    Love said, "You shall be he."
"I, the unkind, ungrateful? Ah, my dear,
    I cannot look on Thee!"   10
Love took my hand and smiling did reply,
    "Who made the eyes but I?"

"Truth, Lord; but I have marred them; let my shame
    Go where it doth deserve."
"And know you not," says Love, "who bore the blame?"   15
    "My dear, then I will serve."
"You must sit down," says Love, "and taste my meat."
    So I did sit and eat.

THE PULLEY

When God at first made man,
Having a glass of blessings standing by,
    "Let us," said he, "pour on him all we can.
Let the world's riches, which dispersed lie,
    Contract into a span."   5

So Strength first made a way;
Then Beauty followed; then Wisdom, Honor, Pleasure.
    When almost all was out, God made a stay,
Perceiving that alone, of all his treasure,
    Rest[1] in the bottom lay.   10

---

1. ease, peace of mind

"For if I should," said he,
"Bestow this jewel also on my creature,
   He would adore my gifts instead of me,
And rest[2] in Nature, not the God of Nature;
   So both should losers be.   15

   "Yet let him keep the rest,[3]
But keep them with repining restlessness;
   Let him be rich and weary, that at least,
If goodness lead him not, yet weariness
   May toss him to my breast."   20

"MY GOD AND KING"

Let all the world in every corner sing,
      My God and King!
   The heavens are not too high,
   His praise may thither fly;
   The earth is not too low,   5
   His praises there may grow.
Let all the world in every corner sing,
      My God and King!

Let all the world in every corner sing,
      My God and King!   10
   The Church with psalms must shout,
   No door can keep them out;
   But, above all, the heart
   Must bear the longest part.
Let all the world in every corner sing,   15
      My God and King!

---

2. take his ease, be content
3. everything else

JOHN MILTON (1608-1674)

ON SHAKESPEARE

What needs my Shakespeare for his honored bones,
The labor of an age in piled stones?
Or that his hallowed reliques should be hid
Under a stary-pointing pyramid?
Dear son of memory, great heir of fame,   5
What need'st thou such weak witness of thy name?
Thou in our wonder and astonishment
Hast built thyself a livelong monument.
For whilst, to the shame of slow-endeavoring art,
Thy easy numbers flow, and that each heart   10
Hath from the leaves of thy unvalued book
Those Delphic lines with deep impression took;
Then thou, our fancy of itself bereaving,
Dost make us marble with too much conceiving,
And so sepulchred in such pomp dost lie   15
That kings for such a tomb would wish to die.

ON THE LATE MASSACRE IN PIEDMONT[1]

Avenge, O Lord, thy slaughtered Saints, whose bones
   Lie scattered on the Alpine mountains cold;
   Even them who kept thy truth so pure of old,
When all our fathers worshiped stocks and stones,
Forget not: in thy book record their groans   5
   Who were thy sheep, and in their ancient fold
   Slain by the bloody Piedmontese, that rolled
Mother with infant down the rocks. Their moans
The vales redoubled to the hills, and they
   To heaven. Their martyred blood and ashes sow   10
O'er all the Italian fields, where still doth sway
The triple Tyrant;[2] that from these may grow
A hundredfold, who, having learnt thy way,
   Early may fly the Babylonian woe.

---

1. The Duke of Savoy had been harassing the Waldenses, a Protestant sect living in northern Italy.
2. the Pope

ON HIS BLINDNESS

When I consider how my light is spent
    Ere half my days[3] in this dark world and wide,
    And that one Talent[4] which is death to hide
Lodged with me useless, though my soul more bent
To serve therewith my Maker, and present   5
    My true account, lest He returning chide;
    "Doth God exact day-labor, light denied?"
I fondly[5] ask. But Patience, to prevent
That murmur, soon replies, "God doth not need
    Either man's work or his own gifts. Who best   10
    Bear his mild yoke, they serve him best. His state
Is kingly: thousands at his bidding speed,
    And post o'er land and ocean without rest;
    They also serve who only stand and wait."

FROM "LYCIDAS"[6]

Yet once more, O ye laurels, and once more,
Ye myrtles brown, with ivy never sere,
I come to pluck your berries harsh and crude,
And with forced fingers rude
Shatter your leaves before the mellowing year.   5
Bitter constraint and sad occasion dear
Compels me to disturb your season due:
For Lycidas[7] is dead, dead ere his prime,
Young Lycidas, and hath not left his peer.
Who would not sing for Lycidas? he knew   10
Himself to sing, and build the lofty rhyme.
He must not float upon his watery bier
Unwept, and welter to the parching wind,
Without the meed of some melodious tear.
    * * * * * * * *

3. He was 44.
4. *Matt.* XXV, 14-30
5. foolishly
6. A lengthy *pastoral elegy* in memory of Edward King, a friend of the young Milton, who drowned in the Irish Sea.
7. Edward King

For we were nursed upon the self-same hill,   15
Fed the same flock by fountain, shade and rill.
Together both, ere the high lawns appeared
Under the opening eye-lids of the Morn,
We drove a-field, and both together heard
What time the gray-fly winds her sultry horn,   20
Battening our flocks with the fresh dews of night;
Oft till the star, that rose at evening bright,
Toward heaven's descent had sloped his westering wheel.
Meanwhile the rural ditties were not mute;
Tempered to the oaten flute,   25
Rough Satyrs danced, and Fauns with cloven heel
From the glad sound would not be absent long;
And old Damoetas loved to hear our song.
    *   *   *   *   *   *   *   *
Bring the rathe primrose that forsaken dies,
The tufted-crow-toe, and pale jessamine,   30
The white pink, and the pansy freaked with jet,
The glowing violet,
The musk-rose, and the well-attired woodbine,
With cowslips wan that hang the pensive head,
And every flower that sad embroidery wears;   35
Bid amaranthus all his beauty shed,
And daffadillies fill their cups with tears
To stew the laureate hearse where Lycid lies.
For so to interpose a little ease,
Let our frail thoughts dally with false surmise.   40
Ay me! whilst thee the shores and sounding seas
Wash far away, — where'er thy bones are hurled;
Whether beyond the stormy Hebrides
Where thou, perhaps, under the whelming tide,
Visitest the bottom of the monstrous world;   45
Or whether thou, to our moist vows denied,
Sleep'st by the fable of Bellerus old,
Where the great vision of the guarded mount
Looks toward Namancos and Bayona's hold —[8]
Look homeward, Angel, now, and melt with ruth: 50
And, O ye dolphins, waft the hapless youth!

Weep no more, woeful shepherds, weep no more,
For Lycidas, your sorrow, is not dead,

---

8.   Reference to a supposed vision of the Archangel Michael on a hill in Cornwall

Sunk though he be beneath the watery floor;
So sinks the day-star in the ocean bed,   55
And yet anon repairs his dropping head,
And tricks his beams, and with new-spangled ore
Flames in the forehead of the morning sky:
So Lycidas sank low, but mounted high
Through the dear might of Him that walked the waves;   60
Where, other groves and other streams along,
With nectar pure his oozy locks he laves,
And hears the unexpressive nuptial song
In the blest kingdoms meek of joy and love.
There entertain him all the saints above   65
In solemn troops, and sweet societies,
That sing, and singing in their glory move,
And wipe the tears forever from his eyes.
Now, Lycidas, the shepherds weep no more;
Henceforth thou art the Genius of the shore   70
In thy large recompense, and shalt be good
To all that wander in that perilous flood.

FROM *PARADISE LOST*

Of Man's first disobedience, and the fruit
Of that forbidden tree whose mortal taste
Brought death into the World, and all our woe,
With loss of Eden, till one greater Man
Restore us, and regain the blissful seat,   5
Sing, Heavenly Muse, that, on the secret top
Of Oreb, or of Sinai, didst inspire
That shepherd[9] who first taught the chosen seed
In the beginning how the heavens and earth
Rose out of Chaos; or, if Sion hill   10
Delight thee more, and Siloa's brook that flowed
Fast by the oracle of God, I thence
Invoke thy aid to my adventurous song,
That with no middle flight intends to soar
Above the Aonian mount,[10] while it pursues   15
Things unattempted yet in prose or rime.

9. Moses
10. Seat of the pagan Muses

And chiefly Thou, O Spirit, that dost prefer
Before all temples the upright heart and pure,
Instruct me, for Thou know'st; Thou from the first
Wast present, and, with mighty wings outspread,   20
Dove-like sat'st brooding on the vast Abyss,
And mad'st it pregnant: what in me is dark
Illumine, what is low raise and support;
That, to the height of this great argument,
I may assert Eternal Providence,   25
And justify the ways of God to men.

 Say first — for Heaven hides nothing from thy view,
Nor the deep tract of Hell — say first what cause
Moved our grand Parents, in that happy state,
Favored of Heaven so highly, to fall off   30
From their Creator, and transgress his will
For one restraint, lords of the World besides.
Who first seduced them to that foul revolt?

 The infernal Serpent; he it was whose guile,
Stirred up with envy and revenge, deceived   35
The mother of mankind, what time his pride
Had cast him out from Heaven, with all his host
Of rebel Angels, by whose aid, aspiring
To set himself in glory above his peers,
He trusted to have equaled the Most High,   40
If he opposed, and, with ambitious aim
Against the throne and monarchy of God,
Raised impious war in Heaven and battle proud,
With vain attempt. Him the Almighty Power
Hurled headlong flaming from the ethereal sky,   45
With hideous ruin and combustion, down
To bottomless perdition, there to dwell
In adamantine chains and penal fire,
Who durst defy the Omnipotent to arms.

 Nine times the space that measures day and night   50
To mortal men, he, with his horrid crew,
Lay vanquished, rolling in the fiery gulf,
Confounded, though immortal. But his doom
Reserved him to more wrath; for now the thought
Both of lost happiness and lasting pain   55

Torments him: round he throws his baleful eyes,
That witnessed huge affliction and dismay,
Mixed with obdurate pride and steadfast hate.
At once, as far as Angels ken, he views
The dismal situation waste and wild. 60
A dungeon horrible, on all sides round,
As one great furnace flamed; yet from those flames
No light; but rather darkness visible
Served only to discover sights of woe,
Reigns of sorrow, doleful shades, where peace 65
And rest can never dwell, hope never comes
That comes to all, but torture without end
Still urges, and a fiery deluge, fed
With ever-burning sulphur unconsumed.
Such place Eternal Justice had prepared 70
For those rebellious; here their prison ordained
In utter darkness, and their portion set,
As far removed from God and light of Heaven
As from the center thrice to the utmost pole.
Oh, how unlike the place from whence they fell! 75
There the companions of his fall, o'erwhelmed
With floods and whirlwinds of tempestuous fire,
He soon discerns; and, weltering by his side,
One next himself in power, and next in crime,
Long after known in Palestine, and named 80
BEELZEBUB. To him the Arch-Enemy,
And thence in Heaven called SATAN, with bold words
Breaking the horrid silence, thus began:—

[Satan attempts to encourage Beelzebub, but finds his chief supporter resigned to the hopelessness of their situation].

Whereto with speedy words the Arch-Fiend replied:—
"Fallen Cherub, to be weak is miserable, 85
Doing or suffering: but of this be sure—
To do aught good never will be our task,
But ever to do ill our sole delight,
As being the contrary to His high will
Whom we resist. If then His providence 90
Out of our evil seek to bring forth good,
Our labor must be to pervert that end,
And out of good still to find means of evil;

Which ofttimes may succeed so as perhaps
Shall grieve Him, if I fail not, and disturb   95
His inmost counsels from their destined aim."

     *   *   *   *   *   *   *   *

   Forthwith upright he rears from off the pool
His mighty stature; on each hand the flames
Driven backward slope their pointing spires, and, rolled
In billows, leave i' the midst a horrid vale.   100
Then with expanded wings he steers his flight
Aloft, incumbent on the dusky air,
That felt unusual weight; till on dry land
He lights—if it were land that ever burned
With solid, as the lake with liquid fire,   105
And such appeared in hue as when the force
Of subterranean wind transports a hill
Torn from Pelorus, or the shattered side
Of thundering Aetna, whose combustible
And fueled entrails, thence conceiving fire,   110
Sublimed with mineral fury, aid the winds,
And leave a singed bottom all involved
With stench and smoke. Such resting found the sole
Of unblest feet. Him followed his next mate;
Both glorying to have 'scaped the Stygian flood   115
As gods, and by their own recovered strength,
Not by the sufferance of supernal power.

   "Is this the region, this the soil, the clime,"
Said then the lost Archangel, "this the seat
That we must change for Heaven?—this mournful gloom   120
For that celestial light? Be it so, since He
Who now is sovran can dispose and bid
What shall be right: farthest from Him is best,
Whom reason hath equaled, force hath made supreme
Above his equals. Farewell, happy fields,   125
Where joy for ever dwells! Hail, horrors! hail,
Infernal World! and thou, profoundest Hell,
Receive thy new possessor—one who brings
A mind not to be changed by place or time.
The mind is its own place, and in itself   130
Can make a Heaven of Hell, a Hell of Heaven.
What matter where, if I still be the same,
And what I should be, all but less than He

Whom thunder hath made greater? Here at least
We shall be free; the Almighty hath not built   135
Here for his envy, will not drive us hence:
Here we may reign secure; and, in my choice,
To reign is worth ambition, though in Hell:
Better to reign in Hell than serve in Heaven."

RICHARD LOVELACE (1618-1658)

TO LUCASTA, ON GOING TO THE WARS

Tell me not, sweet, I am unkind,
    That from the nunnery
Of thy chaste breast and quiet mind
    To war and arms I fly.

True, a new mistress now I chase,   5
    The first foe in the field;
And with a stronger faith embrace
    A sword, a horse, a shield.

Yet this inconstancy is such
    As thou too shalt adore: 10
I could not love thee, dear, so much,
    Loved I not honor more.

TO ALTHEA, FROM PRISON

When Love with unconfined wings
    Hovers within my gates,
And my divine Althea brings
    To whisper at the grates;
When I lie tangled in her hair   5
    And fettered to her eye,
The gods that wanton in the air
    Know no such liberty.

When flowing cups run swiftly round
    With no allaying Thames,[1]   10
Our careless heads with roses bound,
    Our hearts with loyal flames;
When thirsty grief in wine we steep,
    When healths and draughts go free,
Fishes that tipple in the deep   15
    Know no such liberty.

When, like committed linnets, I
    With shriller throat will sing
The sweetness, mercy, majesty,
    And glories of my king;[2]   20
When I shall voice aloud how good
    He is, how great should be,
Enlarged winds, that curl the flood,
    Know no such liberty.

Stone walls do not a prison make,   25
    Nor iron bars a cage:
Minds innocent and quiet take
    That for an hermitage:
If I have freedom in my love,
    And in my soul am free,   30
Angels alone, that soar above,
    Enjoy such liberty.

---

1. *i.e.*, water
2. Lovelace was a very staunch Royalist.

ANDREW MARVELL (1621-1678)

TO HIS COY MISTRESS

Had we but world enough, and time,
This coyness, Lady, were no crime.
We would sit down and think which way
To walk and pass our long love's day.
Thou by the Indian Ganges' side   5
Shouldst rubies find; I by the tide
Of Humber would complain. I would
Love you ten years before the Flood,
And you should, if you please, refuse
Till the conversion of the Jews.   10
My vegetable love should grow
Vaster than empires, and more slow;
An hundred years should go to praise
Thine eyes and on thy forehead gaze;
Two hundred to adore each breast,   15
But thirty thousand to the rest;
An age at least to every part,
And the last age should show your heart.
For, Lady, you deserve this state,
Nor would I love at lower rate.   20
    But at my back I always hear
Time's winged chariot hurrying near;
And yonder all before us lie
Deserts of vast eternity.
Thy beauty shall no more be found,   25
Nor, in thy marble vault, shall sound
My echoing song; then worms shall try
That long preserved virginity,
And your quaint honor turn to dust,
And into ashes all my lust: 30
The grave's a fine and private place,
But none, I think, do there embrace.
    Now therefore, while the youthful hue
Sits on thy skin like morning dew,
And while thy willing soul transpires   35

At every pore with instant fires,
Now let us sport us while we may,
And now, like amorous birds of prey,
Rather at once our time devour
Than languish in his slow-chapped power.   40
Let us roll all our strength and all
Our sweetness up into one ball,
And tear our pleasures with rough strife
Thorough the iron gates of life:
Thus, though we cannot make our sun   45
Stand still, yet we will make him run.

AN EPITAPH

Enough; and leave the rest to Fame!
'Tis to commend her, but to name.
Courtship which, living, she declined,
When dead, to offer were unkind:
Nor can the truest wit, or friend,   5
Without detracting, her commend.
To say—she lived a virgin chaste
In this age loose and all unlaced;
Nor was, when vice is so allowed,
Of virtue or ashamed or proud;   10
That her soul was on Heaven so bent,
No minute but it came and went;
That, ready her last debt to pay,
She summed her life up every day;
Modest as morn, as mid-day bright,   15
Gentle as evening, cool as night:
— 'Tis true; but all too weakly said.
'Twas more significant, she's dead.

HENRY VAUGHAN (1622-1695)

THE WORLD

I saw Eternity the other night,
Like a great ring of pure and endless light,
    All calm, as it was bright;
And round beneath it, Time, in hours, days, years,
    Driv'n by the spheres,   5
Like a vast shadow moved, in which the world
    And all her train were hurled.
The doting lover in his quaintest strain
    Did there complain;
Near him, his lute, his fancy, and his flights,   10
    Wit's sour delights,
With gloves, and knots, the silly snares of pleasure,
    Yet his dear treasure,
All scattered lay, while he his eyes did pour
    Upon a flower.   15

The darksome statesman, hung with weights and woe,
Like a thick midnight-fog, moved there so slow
    He did not stay, nor go;
Condemning thoughts, like sad eclipses, scowl
    Upon his soul,   20
And clouds of crying witnesses without
    Pursued him with one shout.
Yet digged the mole, and, lest his ways be found,
    Worked under ground,
Where he did clutch his prey; but one did see   25
    That policy;
Churches and altars fed him; perjuries
    Were gnats and flies;
It rained about him blood and tears, but he
    Drank them as free.   30

The fearful miser on a heap of rust
Sat pining all his life there, did scarce trust
    His own hands with the dust,

Yet would not place one piece above, but lives
    In fear of thieves.   35
Thousands there were as frantic as himself,
    And hugged each one his pelf;
Tho downright epicure placed heaven in sense,
    And scorned pretence;
While others, slipt into a wide excess,   40
    Said little less;
The weaker sort, slight, trivial wares enslave,
    Who think them brave;
And poor, despised Truth sat counting by
    Their victory.   45

Yet some, who all this while did weep and sing,
And sing and weep, soared up into the ring;
    But most would use no wing.
O fools, said I, thus to prefer dark night
    Before true light!   50
To live in grots and caves, and hate the day
    Because it shows the way,
The way, which from this dead and dark abode
    Leads up to God;
A way where you might tread the sun, and be   55
    More bright than he!
But, as I did their madness so discuss,
    One whispered thus:
"This ring the Bridegroom did for none provide
    But for his bride."   60

VI

THE AGE OF REASON: DRYDEN AND POPE

A wise history teacher once used a homely but effective device to sum up his course in European History. Standing in a large hall before hundreds of students, he tied an eraser to a long string suspended from the ceiling. His initial action was to start it swinging like a giant pendulum; it continued to swing throughout most of his lecture. Hs point was the cyclical nature of history—that revolution is followed by reaction, that noble causes breed cynicism, that times of great tension lead into times of lethargy.

The chief danger in the cyclical view of history is that it is too simple: it suggests that there is but one set of cycles, and it leaves out the exceptions. Actually there tend to be many sets of cycles—little ones within big ones—and there are always exceptions. With a certain extra measure of complexity, however, the idea of cycles in human events is a real aid to the student.

The time now under consideration is a good case in point. Though seventeenth century Englishmen certainly didn't all agree with one another, they shared a habit of disagreeing violently. Whatever their views, they felt strongly about them, and they didn't mind letting their feelings show. And then, quite suddenly, the controversy subsided. It subsided partly because the great issues of the Stuart era were settled. Parliament had won out over the notion of divine right, and that was that. The Anglican Church was to be the Church of England, and that was that. The British Empire was a-building, and the merchants were telling the government how to run it—and that was that.

There was more than just that, however. Men's attitudes changed. They seemed to have had enough conflict; indeed, enough of everything that might make for conflict. Not only was the Crown now subordinate; in the eighteenth century one of its wearers could hardly speak English! Parliament was so much in control that it could be weak; this was a time of governmental lethargy and corruption. In the religious realm, one reason for reduced tension was reduced belief: the highly personal God

of the seventeenth century became a sort of skilled clockmaker who
wound up the universe at the creation and then pretty much left it alone.
This cool and rational semi-religion was called *deism*—and it was highly
influential among intellectual figures of the time. So, if the local parsons
were better at fox-hunting than at theology, nobody really seemed to
care.

This then was a period that had had enough deep feeling, enough
violence. Its tempests were likely to be of teapot size. It prided itself on its
common sense, its rationalism. Its values were harmony, proportion,
grace, balance. It was a time of Georgian architecture, of powdered wigs
and knee britches, of Chippendale furniture, and of the minuet; of highly
polished essays, of the first scientific dictionary, of brilliant literary criticism, and of deft satire. It was not a time of poetry that modern literary
critics receive with any great enthusiasm.

The dearth of poetry can perhaps be explained. Poets are concerned with feeling more than with reason. An age dedicated to avoid-
ance of rocking the boat does not take kindly to obstreporous fellow pass-
engers like passionate poets.

The major literary figure of the Age of Reason was John Dryden
(1631-1700). His depth (or shallowness) of commitment to issues may
be seen in the fact that in 1658 he wrote a poem in praise of the just-
deceased Cromwell; two years later he was writing lavish tributes to
Charles II. But if Dryden was not a deep partisan, or even a sincere one,
he did have the gifts his age was looking for. He was a good playwright,[1]
a fine essayist, and a brilliant literary critic—probably the most brilliant
to write in English up to his time. His poetry is inferior to his criticism—
though polished and competent. Typically of poets of his time, he wrote
mostly in *heroic couplets*—a verse form which emphasizes balance and
proportion at the expense of imagination and excitement. Also typically,
his most congenial subjects were satiric.

If Dryden was the most important literary figure of his day,
Alexander Pope, who came a generation later (1688-1744), was certainly the major poet. In bulk his translations of *The Iliad* and *The
Odyssey* rank largest. They are impressive works; but after the publication of them, Pope is supposed to have been told by a Greek scholar, "A
very pretty translation, Mr. Pope, but it's not Homer." The remark is
revealing as much about Pope's age as about Pope. Homer's values are
not the values of the Age of Reason (which more properly belongs to

---

1. He criticized the Elizabethans for violating the so-called *classical unities,* and was
careful to follow them himself—an indication of the concern of his age for following artistic rules and distrusting imagination and daring.

Horace); Homer is passionate and sometimes rough to the point of crudity. Somehow we can't see Odysseus in a powdered wig.[2]

If Pope had limitations, he also had great strengths. Confining himself almost exclusively to the dominant couplet form, he proved that harmony and proportion need not mean monotony. With great skill he varied the location of the *cesura* in his lines; he saw to it that the stressed syllables had subtle differences in stress; and he managed to provide continuous changes of pace. The beginning poet interested in technique could find few more fruitful models than Alexander Pope.

Pope's subjects, like Dryden's, tended to be satiric; indeed, many of his poems are essays in verse. His most famous poem, *The Rape of the Lock,* is a mock-heroic account of a minor court scandal. While what he said doesn't always seem very "poetic," certainly he always said it with dazzling skill. Few poets are so well represented in dictionaries of familiar quotations.

---

2. Though Macbeth and Hamlet also wore them in eighteenth century performances.

JOHN DRYDEN (1631-1700)

FROM *MAC FLECKNOE*

All human beings are subject to decay,
And when fate summons, monarchs must obey.
This Flecknoe[1] found, who, like Augustus young
Was called to empire, and had governed long;
In prose and verse, was owned, without dispute,   5
Thro' all the realms of *Nonsense,* absolute.
This aged prince, now flourishing in peace,
And blest with issue of a large increase;
Worn out with business, did at length debate
To settle the succession of the State;   10
And, pond'ring which of all his sons was fit
To reign, and wage immortal war with wit,
Cried: "'Tis resolved; for nature pleads, that he
Should only rule, who most resembles me.
Sh——[2] alone my perfect image bears,   15
Mature in dulness from his tender years:
Sh—— alone, of all my sons, is he
Who stands confirmed in full stupidity.
The rest to some faint meaning make pretense,
But Sh—— never deviates into sense.   20
Some beams of wit on other souls may fall,
Strike thro', and make a lucid interval;
But Sh——'s genuine night admits no ray,
His rising fogs prevail upon the day.
Besides, his goodly fabric[3] fills the eye,   25
And seems designed for thoughtless majesty;
Thoughtless as monarch oaks that shade the plain,
And, spread in solemn state, supinely reign.
Heywood and Shirley were but types of thee,
Thou last great prophet of tautology."   30

*   *   *   *   *   *   *   *

---

1. a minor writer
2. Thomas Shadwell, a poet disliked intensely by Dryden
3. Shadwell was a big man

Now Empress Fame had published the renown
Of Sh——'s coronation thro' the town.
Roused by report of Fame, the nations meet
From near Bunhill, and distant Watling Street.
No Persian carpets spread th' imperial way,   35
But scattered limbs of mangled poets lay;
From dusty shops neglected authors come,
Martyrs of pies, and relics of the bum.
Much Heywood, Shirley, Ogleby[4] there lay,
But loads of Sh—— almost choked the way.   40

EPIGRAM ON MILTON

Three poets, in three distant ages born,
Greece, Italy, and England did adorn.
The first[5] in loftiness of thought surpassed,
The next[6] in majesty, in both the last.
The force of Nature could no farther go;   5
To make a third she joined the former two.

ALEXANDER POPE (1688-1744)

FROM *AN ESSAY ON MAN*

   Know then thyself, presume not God to scan,
The proper study of mankind is man.
Placed on this isthmus of a middle state,
A being darkly wise, and rudely great:
With too much knowledge for the sceptic side,   5
With too much weakness for the stoic's pride,
He hangs between; in doubt to act, or rest;
In doubt to deem himself a god, or beast;
In doubt his mind or body to prefer;
Born but to die, and reasoning but to err;   10
Alike in ignorance, his reason such,
Whether he thinks too little or too much:
Chaos of thought and passion, all confused;
Still by himself abused or disabused;

---

4. Three writers of very minor ability, in Dryden's eyes
5. Homer
6. Virgil

Created half to rise and half to fall;   15
Great lord of all things, yet a prey to all;
Sole judge of truth, in endless error hurled:
The glory, jest, and riddle of the world!
     *   *   *   *   *   *   *

   Whate'er the passion—knowledge, fame, or pelf,
No one will change his neighbor with himself.   20
The learned is happy nature to explore,
The fool is happy that he knows no more;
The rich is happy in the plenty given,
The poor contents him with the care of Heaven.
See the blind beggar dance, the cripple sing,   25
The sot a hero, lunatic a king;
The starving chemist in his golden views
Supremely blest, the poet in his muse.
See some strange comfort every state attend,
And pride bestowed on all, a common friend;   30
See some fit passion every age supply,
Hope travels through, nor quits us when we die.

   Behold the child, by nature's kindly law,
Pleased with a rattle, tickled with a straw:
Some livelier play-thing gives his youth delight,   35
A little louder, but as empty quite:
Scarfs, garters, gold, amuse his riper stage,
And beads and prayer-books are the toys of age:
Pleased with this bauble still, as that before;
Till tired he sleeps, and life's poor play is o'er.   40
     *   *   *   *   *   *   *

   Honor and shame from no condition rise;
Act well your part, there all the honor lies.
Fortune in men has some small difference made,
One flaunts in rags, one flutters in brocade;
The cobbler aproned, and the parson gowned,   45
The friar hooded, and the monarch crowned.
"What differ more (you cry) than crown and cowl?"
I'll tell you, friend! a wise man and a fool.
You'll find, if once the monarch acts the monk,
Or, cobbler-like, the parson will be drunk,   50
Worth makes the man, and want of it the fellow;
The rest is all but leather or prunella.[1]

---

1. A cloth used for making parsons' gowns

FROM *AN ESSAY ON CRITICISM*

True ease in writing comes from art, not chance,
As those move easiest who have learned to dance.
'Tis not enough no harshness gives offense,
The sound must seem an echo to the sense.
Soft is the strain when zephyr gently blows,   5
And the smooth stream in smoother numbers flows;
But when loud surges lash the sounding shore,
The hoarse, rough verse should like the torrent roar:
Then Ajax strives some rock's vast weight to throw,
The line too labors, and the words move slow;   10
Not so, when swift Camilla scours the plain,
Flies o'er the unbending corn, and skims along the main.

FROM *EPISTLE TO DR. ARBUTHNOT*

"Shut, shut the door, good John!" fatigued, I said;
"Tie up the knocker, say I'm sick, I'm dead."
The Dog-star rages! nay, 'tis past a doubt
All Bedlam or Parnassus is let out:
Fire in each eye, and papers in each hand,   5
They rave, recite, and madden round the land.

What walls can guard me, or what shades can hide?
They pierce my thickets, thro' my grot they glide,
By land, by water, they renew the charge,
They stop the chariot, and they board the barge.   10
No place is sacred, not the church is free,
Even Sunday shines no Sabbath-day to me:
Then from the Mint[2] walks forth the man of rhyme.
Happy to catch me just at dinner-time.

Is there a Parson much bemused in beer,   15
A maudlin Poetess, a rhyming Peer,
A clerk foredoomed his father's soul to cross,
Who pens a stanza when he should engross?
Is there who, locked from ink and paper, scrawls

2. The Mint was a district in London where debtors could not be arrested by agents
    of their creditors. Since arrest for debt was not permitted on Sunday, debtors at
    that time could safely leave the Mint.

With desperate charcoal round his darkened walls?   20
All fly to TWIT'NAM[3] and in humble strain,
Apply to me to keep them mad or vain.
*   *   *   *   *   *   *   *

  Peace to all such! but were there one[4] whose fires
True Genius kindles, and fair Fame inspires,   25
Blessed with each talent and each art to please,
And born to write, converse, and live with ease;
Should such a man, too fond to rule alone,
Bear, like the Turk, no brother near the throne;
View him with scornful, yet with jealous eyes,   30
And hate for arts that caused himself to rise;
Damn with faint praise, assent with civil leer,
And without sneering teach the rest to sneer;
Willing to wound, and yet afraid to strike,
Just hint a fault, and hesitate dislike;   35
Alike reserved to blame or to commend,
A timorous foe, and a suspicious friend;
Dreading even fools; by flatterers besieged,
And so obliging that he ne'er obliged;
Like Cato, give his little Senate laws,   40
And sit attentive to his own applause:
While Wits and Templars[5] every sentence raise,
And wonder with a foolish face of praise —
Who but must laugh if such a man there be?
Who would not weep, if Atticus[6] were he?   45
*   *   *   *   *   *   *   *

  Yet let me flap this bug[7] with gilded wings,
This painted child of dirt, that stinks and stings;
Whose buzz the witty and the fair annoys,
Yet Wit ne'er tastes, and Beauty ne'er enjoys;
So well-bred spaniels civilly delight   50
In mumbling of the game they dare not bite.
Eternal smiles his emptiness betray,
As shallow streams run dimpling all the way,
Whether in florid impotence he speaks,
And, as the prompter breathes, the puppet squeaks,   55
Or at the ear of Eve, familiar toad,
Half froth, half venom, spits himself abroad,
In puns, or politics, or tales, or lies,

---

3. Twickenham, Pope's estate   6. Addison
4. Joseph Addison, whom Pope disliked   7. Lord Hervey, a bitter enemy
5. law students

Or spite, or smut, or rhymes, or blasphemies;
His wit all see-saw between *that* and *this*,   60
Now high, now low, now master up, now miss,
And he himself one vile Antithesis.
Amphibious thing! that acting either part,
The trifling head, or the corrupted heart;
Fop at the toilet, flatterer at the board,   65
Now trips a lady, and now struts a lord.
Eve's tempter thus the Rabbins have exprest,
A cherub's face, a reptile all the rest;
Beauty that shocks you, Parts that none will trust,
Wit that can creep, and Pride that licks the dust.   70
    * * * * * * * * * *

    Born to no pride, inheriting no strife,
Nor marrying discord in a noble wife,
Stranger to civil and religious rage,
The good man walked innoxious thro' his age.
No courts he saw, no suits would ever try,   75
Nor dared an oath, nor hazarded a lie.
Unlearned, he knew no schoolman's subtle art,[8]
No language but the language of the heart.
By Nature honest, by Experience wise,
Healthy by Temperance and by Exercise;   80
His life, tho' long, to sickness passed unknown,
His death was instant and without a groan.
O grant me thus to live, and thus to die!

---

8. A Roman Catholic, Pope was not permitted to attend a "public" school or a British university. This statement could be a reference to his own rather sketchy education.

VII

THE LATE EIGHTEENTH CENTURY:
PERIOD OF TRANSITION

As the eighteenth century progressed, the pendulum of human events superficially appeared to have ceased swinging. The dominant classes were prosperous and comfortable, in general reluctant to welcome change. One can hardly blame them, for it was a good time to live if one happened to be of the gentlefolk. Few periods have left more handsome remains for later ages to admire. Much of residential London still has an eighteenth century look; so have Edinburgh and Dublin[1]—and surely city houses have never been more pleasing. When the gentry went to play, they took their good taste with them; and the contrast between the spectacular loveliness of eighteenth century Bath and the tawdriness of a nineteenth or twentieth century resort does not argue for continuous improvemnt in human taste. When the gentlman went to his country estate at the end of the London "season," once again he surrounded himself with the aesthetically pleasing. His house would be beautiful, his grounds more so—meticulously tended, formal, park-like. Similar standards governed other arts. The landscapes and portraits of Thomas Gainsborough cannot help but please the eye; even clothing, while perhaps not terribly practical, adorned the human body, male and female, as it has not been adorned since.

The people who enjoyed the fruits of this gracious time also ran the government, and hence not surprisingly the government governed little. The theory seemed to be, ignore unpleasant realities, and perhaps they'll go away. The Kingdom across the Channel ignored them to such an extent that it exploded in 1789. Britain never actually suffered from revolution, but many of the ingredients of revolution were present.

For beneath the fair exterior there was another country, and a far less fair one. A long series of wars with France severely strained the nation's finances, and in a number of ways the burden fell heaviest on

---

1. So, for that matter, have parts of older American cities—Boston, Philadelphia, and Charleston come particularly to mind.

the poor. The landowners discovered that they could recoup their losses by fencing in their estates and raising sheep. Economically this made sense, but it also meant that the tenants, who since human memory had farmed small plots on the estate, no longer could do so. Perhaps they had always in a strict legal sense been landless, but in practice they had always been able to eke out enough to live on. Now, dispossessed, they headed for the cities.

The cities were growing, and not always in ways as pleasing as the town houses of the well-to-do would suggest. A series of inventions, an Empire filled with raw materials, a mercantile economic theory, and a growing landless proletariat combined to build the industrial communities that still mar the green land. This beginning of the *industrial revolution* presented the government with a host of problems, from routine matters like public sanitation to subtler concerns like social disintegration—but few governments could have been less willing or able to cope with them. And so, right outside the gaily lit ballrooms were dark, muddy, stinking streets, inhabited by increasing hordes of increasingly desperate people. Their chief joy was the glass of raw gin, the chief employment of many of them pilferage and robbery. Where there was any official reaction (and most of the time there was not), it tended to be repressive: dozens of crimes were capital, and public hangings were among the more popular recreations of the people. The paintings of Hogarth, which show this side of Britain, provide an interesting contrast with those of Gainsborough.

That there were political figures at least partially aware of circumstances and anxious to deal in fundamental ways with them goes without saying. John Wilkes and Charles James Fox, to name two, were deeply concerned. But a stubborn King (George III), a generally inept Parliament electd from *rotten boroughs,* and simple inertia kept the government from much action until the nineteenth century.

What did all this mean for literature? It meant reactions, of course, for writers are sensitive people, perhaps more likely than most folk to react to things that are amiss. It meant, however, quite often, illogical reactions, partly because writers are no more logical than the rest of us, partly because the problems were unique in human experience, and to this day we have failed to solve them.[2]

One reaction was a curious escape into the weird. Beginning with Horace Walpole's *The Castle of Otranto* (1764), this was the time of the *gothic novel*—tales of beautiful maidens in haunted castles replete with subterranean passages and hidden trap-doors. Walpole himself started a "gothic" fashion by carefully erecting ruins on his estate.

---

2. For example, how many American cities provide a really decent environment for *all* their citizens?

Another escape—at least in literature—was into the country. Its greatest monument is Thomas Gray's "Elegy Written in a Country Churchyard" (1750), where the poet gives an idealized portrait of the generally idyllic life of a village. At a time when the villages were emptying and the smoky cities multiplying, there was undoubted appeal in this sort of writing. Very seldom, though, could writers or readers have guided a plow or milked a cow.

There were genuine cries of anguish, too—but chiefly at growing ugliness and overt cruelty. William Blake bewails the "Satanic Mills" and is outraged by man's inhumanity to man and to lesser creatures—but even he (the greatest poet of the time) failed to realize that most of the cruelty wasn't overt; those responsible for the conduct of affairs were being carried along by a current they didn't understand and possibly were not even aware of. More than individual kindness was needed.

Since many of the social problems of the time seemed to be at base moral, and since the Church, allegedly concerned with morality, appeared to be doing little, it is not surprising that poets should be concerned with the problems of religion. Among other things Blake was a religious poet, burning with a highly personal, mystical vision; and some of the finest religious poetry of any time was written by Christopher Smart. The nature of the times was such that Smart was adjudged insane and committed to an asylum. Clearly, though, the arid deism of the "high and dry"[3] Church of England was insufficient.

These were some of the stirrings beneath the placid surface of eighteenth century England. We refer to their coming to the surface as the Romantic Movement.

---

3. For students of Church history, the term "high" in this context is not the same as "high" in the modern Anglican Church—a term which dates from the Oxford Movement of the nineteenth century. The eighteenth century Church was *socially* "high."

THOMAS GRAY (1716-1771)

ELEGY WRITTEN IN A COUNTRY CHURCHYARD

The curfew tolls the knell of parting day,
  The lowing herd wind slowly o'er the lea,
The ploughman homeward plods his weary way,
And leaves the world to darkness and to me.

Now fades the glimmering landscape on the sight,   5
  And all the air a solemn stillness holds,
Save where the beetle wheels his droning flight,
  And drowsy tinklings lull the distant folds;

Save that from yonder ivy-mantled tower,
  The moping owl does to the moon complain   10
Of such, as wandering near her secret bower,
  Molest her ancient solitary reign.

Beneath those rugged elms, that yew-tree's shade,
  Where heaves the turf in many a moldering heap.
Each in his narrow cell forever laid,   15
  The rude forefathers of the hamlet sleep.

The breezy call of incense-breathing Morn,
  The swallow twittering from the straw-built shed.
The cock's shrill clarion, or the echoing horn,
  No more shall rouse them from their lowly bed.   20

For them no more the blazing hearth shall burn.
  Or busy housewife ply her evening care:
No children run to lisp their sire's return,
  Or climb his knees the envied kiss to share.

Oft did the harvest to their sickle yield,   25
  Their furrow oft the stubborn glebe has broke;
How jocund did they drive their team afield!
  How bowed the woods beneath their sturdy stroke!

Let not Ambition mock their useful toil,
   Their homely joys, and destiny obscure;   30
Nor Grandeur hear with a disdainful smile,
   The short and simple annals of the poor.

The boast of heraldry, the pomp of power,
   And all that beauty, all that wealth e'er gave,
Awaits alike th' inevitable hour: 35
   The paths of glory lead but to the grave.

Nor you, ye proud, impute to these the fault,
   If Memory o'er their tomb no trophies raise,
Where thro' the long-drawn aisle and fretted vault
   The pealing anthem swells the note of praise.   40

Can storied urn or animated bust
   Back to its mansion call the fleeting breath?
Can Honor's voice provoke[1] the silent dust,
   Or Flattery soothe the dull cold ear of Death?

Perhaps in this neglected spot is laid   45
   Some heart once pregnant with celestial fire;
Hands, that the rod of empire might have swayed,
   Or waked to ecstasy the living lyre.

But Knowledge to their eyes her ample page
   Rich with the spoils of time did n'er unroll;   50
Chill Penury repressed their noble rage,
And froze the genial current of the soul.

Full many a gem of purest ray serene
   The dark unfathomed caves of ocean bear:
Full many a flower is born to blush unseen,   55
   And waste its sweetness on the desert air.

Some village-Hampden, that with dauntless breast
   The little tyrant of his fields withstood;
Some mute inglorious Milton here may rest,
   Some Cromwell, guiltless of his country's blood.   60

---

1.   call forth

Th' applause of listening senates to command,
   The threats of pain and ruin to despise,
To scatter plenty o'er a smiling land,
   And read their history in a nation's eyes,

Their lot forbad: nor circumscribed alone   65
   Their growing virtues, but their crimes confined;
Forbad to wade through slaughter to a throne,
   And shut the gates of mercy on mankind;

The struggling pangs of conscious truth to hide,
   To quench the blushes of ingenuous shame,   70
Or heap the shrine of Luxury and Pride
   With incense kindled at the Muse's flame.

Far from the madding crowd's ignoble strife,
   Their sober wishes never learned to stray;
Along the cool sequestered vale of life   75
   They kept the noiseless tenor of their way.

Yet even these bones from insult to protect
   Some frail memorial still erected nigh,
With uncouth rhymes and shapeless sculpture decked,
   Implores the passing tribute of a sigh.   80

Their name, their years, spelt by th' unlettered muse,
   The place of fame and elegy supply:
And many a holy text around she strews,
   That teach the rustic moralist to die.

For who, to dumb Forgetfulness a prey,   85
   This pleasing anxious being e'er resigned,
Left the warm precincts of the cheerful day,
   Nor cast one longing lingering look behind?

On some fond breast the parting soul relies,
   Some pious drops the closing eye requires;   90
Even from the tomb the voice of Nature cries,
   Even in our ashes live their wonted fires.

For thee, who, mindful of th' unhonored dead,
 Dost in these lines their artless tale relate
If chance, by lonely contemplation led,   95
 Some kindred spirit should inquire thy fate, —

Haply some hoary-headed swain may say,
 "Oft have we seen him at the peep of dawn
Brushing with hasty steps the dews away
 To meet the sun upon the upland lawn.   100

"There at the foot of yonder nodding beech
 That wreathes its old fantastic roots so high,
His listless strength at noontide would he stretch,
 And pore upon the brook that babbles by.

"Hard by yon wood, now smiling as in scorn,   105
 Muttering his wayward fancies he would rove;
Now drooping, woeful-wan, like one forlorn,
 Or crazed with care, or crossed in hopeless love.

"One morn I missed him on the customed hill,
 Along the heath and near his favorite tree;   110
Another came; not yet beside the rill,
 Nor up the lawn, nor at the wood was he;

"The next, with dirges due in sad array
 Slow thro' the church-way path we saw him borne; —
Approach and read (for thou canst read) the lay,   115
 Graved on the stone beneath yon aged thorn."

The Epitaph
Here rests his head upon the lap of Earth,
 A Youth, to Fortune and to Fame unknown:
Fair Science frowned not on his humble birth.
 And Melancholy marked him for his own.   120

Large was his bounty, and his soul sincere,
 Heaven did a recompence as largely send:
He gave to Misery all he had, a tear,
 He gained from Heaven ('twas all he wished) a friend.

No farther seek his merits to disclose,   125
  Or draw his frailties from their dread abode,
(There they alike in trembling hope repose,)
  The bosom of his Father and his God.

CHRISTOPHER SMART (1722-71)

FROM *A SONG TO DAVID*

We sing of God, the mighty source
Of all things; the stupendous force
  On which all strength depends;
From whose right arm, beneath whose eyes,
All period, power and enterprise   5
  Commences, reigns, and ends.

The world, the clustering spheres he made,
  The glorious light, the soothing shade,
  Dale, meadow, grove, and hill;
The multitudinous abyss,   10
Where secrecy remains in bliss,
  And wisdom hides her skill.

Glorious the sun in mid career;
Glorious the assembled fires appear;
  Glorious the comet's train;   15
Glorious the trumpet and alarm;
Glorious the almighty stretched-out arm;
  Glorious the enraptured main:

Glorious, most glorious is the crown
Of him that brought salvation down   20
  By meekness, called man's son;
Seers that stupendous truth believed,
And now the matchless deed's achieved,
  Determined, dared, and done.

"O MOST MIGHTY"

O Most Mighty! O Most Holy!
   Far beyond the seraph's thought,
Art thou then so mean and lowly
   As unheeded prophets taught?

O the magnitude of meekness!   5
   Worth from worth immortal sprung;
O the strength of infant weakness,
   If eternal is so young!

God all-bounteous, all-creative
   Whom no ills from good dissuade,   10
Is incarnate, and a native
   Of the very world he made.

OLIVER GOLDSMITH (1730-1774)

FROM *THE DESERTED VILLAGE*

Sweet Auburn! loveliest village of the plain,
Where health and plenty cheered the laboring swain,
Where smiling spring its earliest visit paid,
And parting summer's lingering blooms delayed:
Dear lovely bowers of innocence and ease,   5
Seats of my youth, when every sport could please:
How often have I loitered o'er thy green,
Where humble happiness endeared each scene!
How often have I paused on every charm,
The sheltered cot, the cultivated farm,   10
The never failing brook, the busy mill,
The decent church that topt the neighboring hill,
The hawthorn bush, with seats beneath the shade,
For talking age and whispering lovers made!
How often have I blest the coming day,   15
When toil remitting lent its turn to play,
And all the village train, from labor free,
Led up their sports beneath the spreading tree;

While many a pastime circled in the shade,
The young contending as the old surveyed;   20
And many a gambol frolicked o'er the ground,
And sleights of art and feats of strength went round.
And still, as each repeated pleasure tired,
Succeeding sports the mirthful band inspired;
The dancing pair that simply sought renown,   25
By holding out to tire each other down;
The swain, mistrustless of his smutted face,
While secret laughter tittered round the place;
The bashful virgin's sidelong looks of love,
The matron's glance that would those looks reprove.   30
These were thy charms, sweet village; sports like these,
With sweet succession taught even toil to please;
These round thy bowers their cheerful influence shed,
These were thy charms — but all these charms are fled.

   Sweet smiling village, loveliest of the lawn,   35
Thy sports are fled, and all thy charms withdrawn;
Amidst thy bowers the tyrant's hand is seen,
And desolation saddens all thy green:
One only master grasps the whole domain,
And half a tillage stints thy smiling plain;   40
No more thy glassy brook reflects the day,
But choked with sedges works its weedy way;
Along thy glades, a solitary guest,
The hollow-sounding bittern guards its nest;
Amidst thy desert walks the lapwing flies,   45
And tires their echoes with unvaried cries.
Sunk are thy bowers in shapeless ruin all,
And the long grass o'ertops the mouldering wall;
And, trembling, shrinking from the spoiler's hand,
Far, far away thy children leave the land.   50

   Ill fares the land, to hastening ills a prey,
Where wealth accumulates, and men decay;
Princes and lords may flourish, or may fade;
A breath can make them, as a breath has made;
But a bold peasantry, their country's pride,   55
When once destroyed, can never be supplied.

WILLIAM BLAKE (1757-1827)

THE LITTLE BLACK BOY

My mother bore me in the southern wild,
   And I am black, but O my soul is white!
White as an angel is the English child,
   But I am black, as if bereaved of light.

My mother taught me underneath a tree,   5
   And, sitting down before the heat of day,
She took me on her lap and kissèd me,
   And, pointing to the east, began to say:

"Look at the rising sun; — there God does live,
   And gives His light, and gives His heat away;   10
And flowers and trees and beasts and men receive
   Comfort in morning, joy in the noonday.

"And we are put on earth, a little space,
   That we may learn to bear the beams of love;
And these black bodies and this sunburnt face   15
   Is but a cloud, and like a shady grove.

"For when our souls have learned the heat to bear,
   The cloud will vanish, we shall hear His voice,
Saying: 'Come out from the grove, my love and care,
   And round my golden tent like lambs rejoice.' "   20

Thus did my mother say, and kissèd me;
   And thus I say to little English boy,
When I from black, and he from white cloud free,
   And round the tent of God like lambs we joy,

I'll shade him from the heat, till he can bear   25
   To lean in joy upon our Father's knee;
And then I'll stand and stroke his silver hair,
   And be like him, and he will then love me.

THE TIGER

Tiger! Tiger! burning bright
In the forests of the night,
What immortal hand or eye
Could frame thy fearful symmetry?

In what distant deeps or skies   5
Burnt the fire of thine eyes?
On what wings dare he aspire?
What the hand dare seize the fire?

And what shoulder, and whart art,
Could twist the sinews of thy heart?   10
And when thy heart began to beat,
What dread hand and what dread feet?

What the hammer? what the chain?
In what furnace was thy brain?
What the anvil? what dread grasp   15
Dare its deadly terrors clasp?

When the stars threw down their spears,
And watered heaven iwth their tears,
Did He smile his work to see?
Did He who made the Lamb make thee?   20

Tiger! Tiger! burning bright,
In the forests of the night,
What immortal hand or eye
Dare frame thy fearful symmetry?

THE CLOD AND THE PEBBLE

"Love seeketh not itself to please,
    Nor for itself hath any care,
But for another gives its ease,
    And builds a Heaven in Hell's despair."

So sung a little clod of clay,   5
    Trodden with the cattle's feet,
But a pebble of the brook
    Warbled out these metres meet:

"Love seeketh only Self to please,
   To bind another to its delight,   10
Joys in another's loss of ease,
   And builds a Hell in Heaven's despite."

STANZAS FROM *MILTON*

And did those feet in ancient time
   Walk upon England's mountains green?
And was the holy Lamb of God
   On England's pleasant pastures seen?

And did the Countenance Divine   5
   Shine forth upon our clouded hills?
And was Jerusalem builded here
   Among these dark Satanic mills?

Bring me my bow of burning gold!
   Bring me my arrows of desire!   10
Bring me my spear! O clouds, unfold!
   Bring me my chariot of fire!

I will not cease from mental fight,
   Nor shall my sword sleep in my hand,
Till we have built Jerusalem   15
   In England's green and pleasant land.

THE SICK ROSE

   O rose, thou art sick:
   The invisible worm
   That flies in the night,
   In the howling storm,

   Has found out thy bed   5
   Of crimson joy,
   And his dark secret love
   Does thy life destroy.

THE SUNFLOWER

Ah, Sunflower, weary of time,
Who countest the steps of the Sun,
Seeking after that sweet golden clime
Where the traveler's journey is done:

Where the Youth pined away with desire,   5
And the pale Virgin shrouded in snow,
Arise from their graves, and aspire
Where my Sunflower wishes to go.

FROM *AUGURIES OF INNOCENCE*

To see a world in a grain of sand
And a Heaven in a wild flower,
Hold Infinity in the palm of your hand
And Eternity in an hour.

A robin redbreast in a cage   5
Puts all Heaven in a rage.
A dove-house filled with doves and pigeons
Shudders Hell through all its regions.
A dog starved at his master's gate
Predicts the ruin of the state.   10
A horse misused upon the road
Calls to Heaven for human blood.
Each outcry of the hunted hare
A fibre from the brain does tear.
A skylark wounded in the wing,   15
A cherubim does cease to sing.
The game cock clipped and armed for fight
Does the rising sun affright.
Every wolf's and lion's howl
Raises from Hell a human soul.   20
The wild deer wandering here and there
Keeps the human soul from care.
The lamb misused breeds public strife
And yet forgives the butcher's knife.
The bat that flits at close of eve   25
Has left the brain that won't believe.
The owl that calls upon the night
Speaks the unbeliever's fright.
     *   *   *   *   *   *   *   *
The wanton boy that kills the fly
Shall feel the spider's enmity.   30
He who torments the chafer's sprite
Weaves a bower in endless night.

The caterpillar on the leaf
Repeats to thee thy mother's grief.
Kill not the moth nor butterfly   35
For the Last Judgment draweth nigh.
          *   *   *   *   *   *   *   *
He who mocks the infant's faith
Shall be mocked in Age and Death.
He who shall teach the child to doubt
The rotting grave shall ne'er get out.   40
He who respects the infant's faith
Triumphs over Hell and Death.
          *   *   *   *   *   *   *   *
He who doubts from what he sees
Will ne'er believe, do what you please.
If the sun and moon should doubt,   45
They'd immediately go out.

To be in a passion you good may do,
But no good if a passion is in you.

The whore and gambler, by the state
Licenced, build that nation's fate.   50
The harlot's cry from street to street
Shall weave Old England's winding sheet.
          *   *   *   *   *   *   *   *
God appears, and God is Light
To those poor souls who dwell in night,
But does a human form display   55
To those who dwell in realms of day.

VIII

THE ROMANTIC MOVEMENT

The Romantic Movement was possibly as spectacular an artistic outpouring as the world has seen. If the English-speaking lands would perhaps give supremacy to the Elizabethans, it must be remembered that the Romantic Movement embraced all Western Civilizaton, not just the part of it that spoke English. Involved in Romanticism were such diverse items as Greek independence, Beethoven, Napoleon, *Moby Dick,* and the Great Reform Bill.

Because Romanticism was both many-faceted and dramatic, it is extremely hard to define. The dramatic elements are easily noted, but they tend to contradict one another because of the complexity of the Movement as a whole. For example, one aspect of Romanticism clearly was political liberalism. The French Revolution was its child, and Lord Byron died in the Greek revolt agains the Ottoman Empire. Yet the mature Wordsworth (after a brief youthful fling at liberalism) was a staunch tory — and one of the great Romantic poets. For another example, Lord Byron is lumped together with about half a dozen other poets whom we refer to as the English Romantics. And yet Byron cordially detested Wordsworth, Coleridge, and Southey, admired Pope enormously, and certainly would have been appalled at the thought that a later generation would list him as it has.

Romanticism has been further confused by becoming subject to clichés. We are told that Romantic writers were interested in nature. Yet almost immediately we find some Romantic poets (such at Keats) spending very little time describing nature; and we find further that poets, like everyone else, have always been "interested" in nature. The cliché has a piece of truth: interest in nature *is* important in Romanticism. But first the kind of interest must be explained, and then the usual exceptions must be allowed for.

Remembering the image of the swinging pendulum, we might define Romanticism as a giant reaction—political, social, and artistic—against everything that had been before: illiberal governments, static societies, and arts bound by rules. The eighteenth century had swept a lot under the rug; Romanticism gave the rug a cosmic shake.

When the student comes to Romantic traits and attitudes, he should remember (as has already been said) that the Movement was too diverse for any one figure to embody everything that was Romantic. Certainly no person could be called Romantic who did not embody *some* of tht characteristics of Romanticism; but some only, not all.

There follow some of the more important characteristics of Romanticism:

(1) An appreciation of nature as the surest vehicle in which to approach the Source of nature. Wordsworth wrote:

> . . . I have felt
> A presence that disturbes me with the joy
> Of elevated thoughts; a sence sublime
> Of something far more deeply interfused,
> Whose dwelling is the light of setting suns,
> And the round ocean and the living air,
> And the blue sky, and in the mind of man;
> A motion and a spirit, that impels
> All thinking things, all objects of all thought,
> And rolls through all things.

He seems to be saying that the Creator is best reached through the beauties of the natural creation. This mystical feeling for nature is far different from the uncomplicated delight in lovely scenery that is found in, say, Shakespeare and Herrick, and even more different from the Augustan enthusiasm for "tame nature," for neatly landscaped parks and estates.

Wordsworth, the greatest "nature poet" in English, manages to keep the distinction between God and nature, however useful the latter may be to approach the former. A characteristic of some Romantic writers, however, is to blur the distinction: with Emerson, for example, nature seems almost to *become* God.

(2) Political liberalism. The eighteenth century rulers in general resisted change; there was a great deal of political unfinished business in Europe. Until the defeat of Napoleon, English Romantics were caught in something of a bind: they were all for his breaking up of antique and antiquated continental states, but at the same time their country was almost continuously at war with him. After Waterloo the chief political goal of the English liberals was reform of the suffrage. Some of the "rotten boroughs" had more representatives in Parliament than voters, while new industrial cities like Manchester and Birmingham had no representatives at all. Another major goal in both England and America was the abolition of slavery.

(3) Interest in the common man. This point is obviously related to the preceding one. The previous century had been strong on ceremonial and the social rigidity that tends to go with it. Now there was a reaction: "A man's a man for a' that," wrote Robert Burns — and the unadorned man became worth writing about. While writing about ordinary people, some Romantic writers also urged the substitution of everyday language for the "special" diction usually associated with poetry.

(4) The long ago and far away. Again, something of a reaction. Exotic adventure played a rather small role on the eighteenth century stage. Satire, the great literary technique of the time, almost by definition deals with the present. The Romantic story-teller tended to move to "romantic" (lower case) topics.

(5) Interest in the weird and supernatural. Almost a continuation of point No. 4. The gothic novel of the late eighteenth century carried over into a rather more serious concern in Romanticism. Coleridge, the great poet of the supernatural, did not use it as a mere prop to enliven his tales; he was seriously interested in the interaction of natural and supernatural.

(6) Artistic experimentation. The eighteenth century artist lived by the rules; the Romantic threw them off. In poetry the unshackling manifested itself in the use of dozens of different verse forms. In place of harmony, proportion, grace, and balance the Romantic poet extolled brilliance, excitement, emotional content — even shock.

(7) Above all, imagination. The eighteenth century distrusted it; the Romanticists almost deified it. Speaking of Fancy (his synonym for imagination), Keats wrote:

> Open wide the mind's cage-door,
> She'll dart forth, and cloudward soar.
> O sweet Fancy! let her loose. . . .

Perhaps these three lines will define the Romantic spirit as well as any.

A word now about the dates of Romanticism and a few comments on the major Romantic poets. Although in retrospect Romanticism seems to have seized men's minds more quickly and dramatically than most movements, those involved in it didn't suddenly wake up one morning, apprehend a revelation, and say, "The Romantic era has arrived; we will now all be different." As a political phenomenon Romanticism has roots at least as far back as the Declaration of Independence. Jefferson's guide may have been none other than rational old John Locke, then well over fifty years dead — but the Jeffersonian treatment of Locke's ideas was highly Romantic. So was Jean-Jacques Rousseau, whose *Contrat Social* dates from 1762. The "gothic" element in Romanticism, as we have seen, also began well back in the eighteenth century.

Still, these were beginnings, not the culmination. Probably the best dates for the start of Romanticism are either 1789, the French Revolution, or 1798, the publication date of *Lyrical Ballads* by Wordsworth and Coleridge, the first literary work which specifically and self-consciously announced itself to be "different" — the harbinger of a new era.

In one sense the Romantic period has never ended; much contemporary popular entertainment is Romantic. As a serious intellectual trend, however, it was a phenomenon of the early nineteenth century. In Britain it certainly did not outlast Wordsworth (who died in 1850); in the United States, where there was a "cultural lag" behind Britain throughout much of the century, it held on longer — certainly through the major poems of Walt Whitman (all written by about 1870).

There are generally considered to be five major English Romantic poets; significant also are a Scotsman (Burns) and two Americans (Emerson and Poe).

William Wordsworth was above all the poet of nature. He was the best-known of the "Lake Poets," who took their name from their residence in the Lake District of northwestern England. While Wordsworth's nature has a picture-postcard quality to it, and he never seems to get his hands dirty, there is no denying the splendor of his descriptions or the genuine feeling behind his mystical relationship with the natural creation.

A close friend of Wordsworth was Samuel Taylor Coleridge. Perhaps the deepest thinker among the English-speaking Romantics, he had various personal weaknesses which seriously hurt his poetry. Dogged with ill health, he too frequently had recourse to what he euphemistically called an "anodyne." One result was a chronic inability to finish poems; only one major poem ("The Rime of the Ancient Mariner") is complete. Coleridge excelled in the weird and haunted aspect of Romanticism.

A generation separated Wordsworth and Coleridge from the three other major English poets of the Movement, all of whom had short lives and who consequently always seem very young. George Gordon, Lord Byron, was perhaps more "romantic" than Romantic: a dashing, swashbuckling sort of fellow, renowned as a great lover. He exiled himself from Britain in protest against what he regarded as excessively stuffy British social and moral standards. Though much of his best poetry has an eighteenth century satiric tone to it (plus humor — welcome in a rather overly solemn period), he is Romantic in his feeling for scenery, his sense of adventure, his delight in the long ago and far away, and his dislike of restraints. Though much of his life must be regarded as not entirely creditable, he literally gave his all to the cause of Greek independence, dying of a fever he contracted while serving with the insurgents.

Percy Bysshe Shelley was the classic radical. He was expelled from Oxford for circulating a pamphlet entitled "The Necessity of Atheism." He married a sixteen-year-old girl whom he subsequently left; after she drowned herself there was considerable outcry in England, and Shelley, like Byron, became an exile. He married Mary Godwin, daughter of an anarchist philosopher and herself the author of *Frankenstein*. His career abruptly ended when a small boat in which he was sailing capsized in the Mediterranean.

For all his eccentric behavior Shelley was a lovable person, outraged about what he regarded as cant and hypocrisy. A loyal friend, he was extremely helpful to his brother poet, John Keats. Shelley is Romantic in his passion for liberty, his depth of feeling, and his experimentation in verse; this last quality has made him something of a "poet's poet."

Perhaps the greatest Romantic poet was John Keats. Like Byron and Shelley he died away from England, but in his case for reasons of health. He was a victim of tuberculosis, then incurable, and had gone to Italy in hopes that warmth and sunshine would prolong his life.

Keats was a poor boy — one of the earliest such to become a major poet. His father kept a livery stable; he himself became a surgeon (then a profession of no distinction), but abandoned his trade for literature. Throughout his writing there runs a thread of discovery — the reaction of a deprived youth continuously discovering the wonders of the world. Keats is hard to characterize, but above all else he is the poet of imagination. He also writes with a unique and most thoroughly Romantic richness and splendor of imagery.

The role of Robert Burns is difficult to assess. In Scotland he is now a national institution, but he had no particular influence on other poets during his lifetime. Born to poverty, and never very far from it, he was perhaps a Romantic without knowing it, though he wrote earlier than the "official" Romantic poets. His best poems tell about the simple peasant life he himself knew, written usually in a Scots dialect whose delightful atmosphere makes up for a certain difficulty of comprehension.

America before the Civil War for a variety of reasons was not in a position to support many men of letters, but two Romantic poets are worth noting. Ralph Waldo Emerson was clumsy in his technique, but he represented many of the Wordsworthian aspects of Romanticism. Edgar Allan Poe, plagued all his life by personal misfortune and poverty, felt that poetry need not say anything meaningful as long as it had emotional content. His best poems do have this quality, though he was forced by economic pressures to write far too much for uniform high quality.

ROBERT BURNS (1759-1796)

TO A MOUSE
On Turning Her up in Her
Nest with the Plough, November, 1785

Wee, sleekit, cowrin, tim'rous beastie,
O, what a panic's in thy breastie!
Thou need na start awa sae hasty
    Wi' bickering brattle![1]
I wad be laith to rin an' chase thee,   5
    Wi' murdering pattle![2]

I'm truly sorry man's dominion
Has broken Nature's social union,
An' justifies that ill opinion
    Which makes thee startle   10
At me, thy poor, earth-born companion
    An' fellow mortal!

I doubt na, whyles, but thou may thieve;
What then? poor beastie, thou maun live!
A daimen icker in a thrave[3]
    'S a sma' request;
I'll get a blessin wi' the lave,
    An' never miss 't!

Thy wee-bit housie, too, in ruin!
It's silly wa's the win's are strewin!   20
An' naething, now, to big a new ane,
    O' foggage green!
An' bleak December's win's ensuin,
    Baith snell[4] an' keen!

---

1. hurrying scamper
2. spade
3. an occasional ear in a bundle of sheaves
4. biting

Thou saw the fields laid bare an' waste,
An' weary winter comin fast,
An' cozie here, beneath the blast,
    Thou thought to dwell,
Till crash! the cruel coulter[5] past
    Out thro' thy cell   30

That wee bit heap o' leaves an' stibble,
Has cost thee monie a weary nibble!
Now thou's turned out, for a' thy trouble,
    But house or hald,[6]
To thole[7] the winter's sleety dribble,   35
    An' cranreuch[8] cauld!

But Mouise, thou art no thy lane,
In proving foresight may be vain;
The best-laid schemes o' mice an' men
    Gang aft agley,[9]   40
An' lea'e us nought but grief an' pain,
    For promised joy!

Still thou art blest, compared wi' me!
The present only toucheth thee:
But och! I backward cast my e'e,   45
    On prospects drear!
An' forward, tho' I canna see,
    I guess an' fear!

"SCOTS, WHA HAE"

Scots, wha hae wi' Wallace bled,
Scots, wham Bruce has aften led,
Welcome to your gory bed
    Or to victorie!

Now's the day, and now's the hour: 5
See the front o' battle lour,
See approach proud Edward's power —
    Chains and slaverie!

5. plow
6. without house or property
7. endure
8. hoar-frost
9. askew

Wha will be a traitor knave?
Wha will fill a coward's grave?   10
What sae base as be a slave? —
    Let him turn, and flee!

Wha for Scotland's King and Law
Freedom's sword will strongly draw,
Freeman stand or freeman fa',   15
    Let him follow me!

By Oppression's woes and pains,
By your sons in servile chains,
We will drain our deepest veins
    But they shall be free!   20

Lay the proud usurpers low!
Tyrants fall in every foe!
Liberty's in every blow!
    Let us do, or die!

"IS THERE FOR HONEST POVERTY"

Is there for honest poverty
    That hangs his head, an' a' that?
The coward slave, we pass him by —
    We dare be poor for a' that!
For a' that, an' a' that,   5
    Our toils obscure, an' a' that,
The rank is but the guinea's stamp,
    The man's the gowd[10] for a 'that.

What though on hamely fare we dine,
    Wear hoddin[11] grey, an' a' that?   10
Gie fools their silks, and knaves their wine —
    A man's a man for a' that.
For a' that, an' a' that,
    Their tinsel show, an' a' that,
The honest man, tho' e'er sae poor,   15
    Is king o' men for a' that.

---

10. gold
11. homespun

Ye see yon birkie[12] ca'd a lord,
   Wha struts, an' stares, an' a' that?
Tho' hundreds worship at his word,
   He's but a cuif[13] for a' that.   20
For a' that, an' a' that,
   His ribband, star, an' a' that,
The man o' independent mind,
   He looks an' laughs at a' that.

A prince can make a belted knight,   25
   A marquis, duke, an' a' that!
But an honest man's aboon[14] his might —
   Guid faith, he mauna fa'[15] that!
For a' that, an' a' that,
   Their dignities, an' a' that,   30
The pith o' sense an' pride o' worth
   Are higher rank than a' that.

Then let us pray that come it may
   (As come it will for a' that)
That Sense and Worth o'er a' the earth   35
   Shall bear the gree[16] an' a' that!
For a' that, an' a' that,
   It's comin yet for a' that,
That man to man the world o'er
   Shall brithers be for a' that.   40

---

12. fellow   15. claim
13. ninny   16. take first place
14. above

WILLIAM WORDSWORTH (1770-1850)

LINES

Composed a Few Miles Above Tintern Abbey, on Revisiting the Banks of the Wye During a Tour, July 13, 1798

Five years have passed; five summers, with the length
Of five long winters! and again I hear
These waters, rolling from their mountain-springs
With a soft inland murmur. — Once again
Do I behold these steep and lofty cliffs,   5

That on a wild, secluded scene impress
Thoughts of more deep seclusion; and connect
The landscape with the quiet of the sky.
The day is come when I again repose
Here, under this dark sycamore, and view   10
These plots of cottage-ground, these orchard-tufts,
Which at this season, with their unripe fruits,
Are clad in one green hue, and lose themselves
'Mid groves and copses. Once again I see
These hedge-rows, hardly hedge-rows, little lines   15
Of sportive wood run wild: these pastoral farms,
Green to the very door; and wreaths of smoke
Sent up, in silence, from among the trees!
With some uncertain notice, as might seem
Of vagrant dwellers in these houseless woods,   20
Or of some Hermit's cave, where by his fire
The Hermit sits alone.

              These beauteous forms,
Through a long absence, have not been to me
As a landscape to a blind man's eye:
But oft, in lonely rooms, and 'mid the din   25
Of towns and cities, I have owed to them,
In hours of weariness, sensations sweet,
Felt in the blood, and felt along the heart;
And passing even into my purer mind,
With tranquil restoration: — feelings too   30
Of unremembered pleasure: such, perhaps,
As have no slight or trivial influence
On that best portion of a good man's life,
His little, nameless, unremembered acts
Of kindness and of love. Nor less, I trust,   35
To them I may have owed another gift,
Of aspect more sublime; that blessed mood
In which the burden of the mystery,
In which the heavy and the weary weight
Of all this unintelligible world,   40
Is lightened: — that serene and blessed mood,
In which the affections gently lead us on, —
Until, the breath of this corporeal frame
And even the motion of our human blood
Almost suspended, we are laid asleep   45

In body, and become a living soul:
While with an eye made quiet by the power
Of harmony, and the deep power of joy,
We see into the life of things.

                                    If this
Be but a vain belief, yet, oh! how oft —   50
In darkness and amid the many shapes
Of joyless daylight; when the fretful stir
Unprofitable, and the fever of the world,
Have hung upon the beatings of my heart —
How oft, in spirit, have I turned to thee,   55
O sylvan Wye! thou wanderer thro' the woods,
How often has my spirit turned to thee!

And now, with gleams of half-extinguished thought,
With many recognitions dim and faint,
And somewhat of a sad perplexity   60
The picture of the mind revives again:
While here I stand, not only with the sense
Of present pleasure, but with pleasing thoughts
That in this moment there is life and food
For future years, And so I dare to hope,   65
Though changed, no doubt, from what I was when first
I came among these hills; when like a roe
I bounded o'er the mountains, by the sides
Of the deep rivers, and the lonely streams,
Wherever nature led: more like a man   70
Flying from something that he dreads, than one
Who sought the thing he loved. For nature then
(The coarser pleasures of my boyish days,
And their glad animal movements all gone by)
To me was all in all. — I cannot paint   75
What then I was. The sounding cataract
Haunted me like a passion: the tall rock,
The mountain, and the deep and gloomy wood,
Their colors and their forms, were then to me
An appetite; a feeling and a love,   80
That had no need of a remoter charm,
By thought supplied, nor any interest
Unborrowed from the eye. — That time is past,
And all its aching joys are now no more,

And all its dizzy reptures. Not for this   85
Faint I, nor mourn nor murmur; other gifts
Have followed; for such loss, I would believe,
Abundant recompense. For I have learned
To look on nature, not as in the hour
Of thoughtless youth; but hearing oftentimes   90
The still, sad music of humanity,
Nor harsh nor grating, though of ample power
To chasten and subdue. And I have felt
A presence that disturbs me with the joy
Of elevated thoughts; a sense sublime   95
Of something far more deeply interfused,
Whose dwelling is the light of setting suns,
And the round ocean and the living air,
And the blue sky, and in the mind of man;
A motion and a spirit, that impels   100
All thinking things, all objects of all thought,
And rolls through all things. Therefore am I still
A lover of the meadows and the woods,
And mountains; and of all that we behold
From this green earth; of all the mighty world   105
Of eye, and ear, — both what they half create,
And what perceive; well pleased to recognize
In nature and the language of the sense
The anchor of my purest thoughts, the nurse,
The guide, the guardian of my heart, and soul   110
Of all my moral being.

                              Nor perchance,
If I were not thus taught, should I the more
Suffer my genial spirits, to decay:
For thou[1] art with me here upon the banks
Of this fair river; thou my dearest Friend,   115
My dear, dear Friend; and in thy voice I catch
The language of my former heart, and read
My former pleasures in the shooting lights
Of thy wild eyes. Oh! yet a little while
May I behold in thee what I was once,   120
My dear, dear Sister! and this prayer I make,
Knowing that Nature never did betray

---

1. his sister, Dorothy

The heart that loved her; 'tis her privilege,
Through all the years of this our life, to lead
From joy to joy: for she can so inform   125
The mind that is within us, so impress
With quietness and beauty, and so feed
With lofty thoughts, that neither evil tongues,
Rash judgments, nor the sneers of selfish men,
Nor greetings where no kindness is, nor all   130
The dreary intercourse of daily life,
Shall e'er prevail against us, or disturb
Our cheerful faith, that all which we behold
Is full of blessings. Therefore let the moon
Shine on thee in thy solitary walk;   135
And let the misty mountain-winds be free
To blow against thee: and, in after years,
When these wild ecstasies shall be matured
Into a sober pleasure; when thy mind
Shall be a mansion for all lovely forms,   140
Thy memory be as a dwelling-place
For all sweet sounds and harmonies; oh! then,
If solitude, or fear, or pain, or grief,
Should be thy portion, with what healing thoughts
Of tender joy wilt thou remember me,   145
And these my exhortations! Nor, perchance —
If I should be where I no more can hear
Thy voice, nor catch from thy wild eyes these gleams
Of past existence — wilt thou then forget
That on the banks of this delightful stream   150
We stood together; and that I, so long
A worshiper of Nature, hither came
Unwearied in that service: rather say
With warmer love — oh! with far deeper zeal
Of holier love. Nor wilt thou then forget,   155
That after many wanderings, many years
Of absence, these steep woods and lofty cliffs,
And this green pastoral landscape, were to me
More dear, both for themselves and for thy sake!

"MY HEART LEAPS UP"

My heart leaps up when I behold
   A rainbow in the sky:
So was it when my life began,
So is it now I am a man,
So be it when I shall grow old,   5
   Or let me die!
The Child is father of the Man:
And I could wish my days to be
Bound each to each by natural piety.

"IT IS A BEAUTEOUS EVENING"

It is a beauteous evening, calm and free;
The holy time is quiet as a Nun
Breathless with adoration; the broad sun
Is sinking down in its tranquility;
The gentleness of heaven broods o'er the Sea: 5
Listen, the mighty Being is awake,
And doth with his eternal motion make
A sound like thunder — everlastingly.
Dear Child![2] dear Girl! that walkest with me here,
If thou appear untouched by solemn thought,   10
Thy nature is not therefore less divine:
Thou liest in Abraham's bosom all the year;
And worship'st at the Temple's inner shrine,
God being with thee when we know it not.

LONDON, 1802

Milton! thou shouldst be living at this hour:
England hath need of thee: she is a fen
Of stagnant waters: altar, sword, and pen,
Fireside, the heroic wealth of hall and bower,
Have forfeited their ancient English dower   5
Of inward happiness. We are selfish men:
Oh! raise us up, return to us again;
And give us manners, virtue, freedom, power.

---

2. his daughter

Thy soul was like a Star, and dwelt apart:
Thou hadst a voice whose sound was like the sea,   10
Pure as the naked heavens, majestic, free;
So didst thou travel on life's common way
In cheerful godliness; and yet thy heart
The lowliest duties on herself did lay.

"THE WORLD IS TOO MUCH WITH US"

The world is too much with us; late and soon,
Getting and spending, we lay waste our powers:
Little we see in Nature that is ours;
We have given our hearts away, a sordid boon!
The Sea that bares her bosom to the moon;   5
The winds that will be howling at all hours
And are up-gathered now like sleeping flowers;
For this, for every thing, we are out of tune;
It moves us not. — Great God! I'd rather be
A Pagan suckled in a creed outworn;   10
So might I, standing on this pleasant lea,
Have glimpses that would make me less forlorn;
Have sight of Proteus rising from the sea;
Or hear old Triton blow his wreathed horn.

FROM *ODE ON INTIMATIONS OF IMMORTALITY*

Our birth is but a sleep and a forgetting;
The Soul that rises with us, our life's Star,
        Hath had elsewhere its setting,
            And cometh from afar;
        Not in entire forgetfulness,   5
        And not in utter nakedness,
But trailing clouds of glory do we come
            From God, who is our home:
Heaven lies about us in our infancy!
Shades of the prison-house begin to close   10
        Upon the growing Boy,
But he beholds the light, and whence it flows,
        He sees it in his joy;

The Youth, who daily farther from the east
    Must travel, still is Nature's priest,   15
        And by the vision splendid
        Is on his way attended;
At length the Man perceives it die away,
And fade into the light of common day.

SAMUEL TAYLOR COLERIDGE (1772-1834)

KUBLA KHAN

    In Xanadu did Kubla Khan
    A stately pleasure-dome decree:
    Where Alph, the sacred river, ran
    Through caverns measureless to man
        Down to a sunless sea.   5
So twice five miles of fertile ground
With walls and towers were girdled around:
And here were gardens bright with sinuous rills,
Where blossomed many an incense-bearing tree;
And here were forests ancient as the hills,   10
Enfolding sunny spots of greenery.

But oh! that deep romantic chasm which slanted
Down the green hill athwart a cedarn cover!
A savage place! as holy and enchanted
As e'er beneath a waning moon was haunted   15
By woman wailing for her demon-lover!
And from this chasm, with ceaseless turmoil seething,
As if this earth in fast thick pants were breathing,
A mighty fountain momently was forced;
Amid whose swift half-intermitted burst   20
Huge fragments vaulted like rebounding hail,
Or chaffy grain beneath the thresher's flail:
And 'mid these dancing rocks at once and ever
It flung up momently the sacred river.
Five miles meandering with a mazy motion   25
Through wood and dale the sacred river ran,

Then reached the caverns measureless to man,
And sank in tumult to a lifeless ocean:
And 'mid this tumult Kubla heard from far
Ancestral voices prophesying war!   30

    The shadow of the dome of pleasure
    Floated midway on the waves;
    Where was heard the mingled measure
    From the fountain and the caves.
    It was a miracle of rare device,   35
    A sunny pleasure-dome with caves of ice!

    A damsel with a dulcimer
    In a vision once I saw:
    It was an Abyssinian maid,
    And on her dulcimer she played,   40
    Singing of Mount Abora.
    Could I revive within me,
    Her symphony and song,
    To such a deep delight 'twould win me,
That with music loud and long,   45
I would build that dome in air,
That sunny dome! those caves of ice!
And all who heard should see them there,
And all should cry, Beware! Beware!
His flashing eyes, his floating hair!   50
Weave a circle round him thrice,
And close your eyes with holy dread,
For he on honey-dew hath fed,
And drunk the milk of Paradise.

THE RIME OF THE ANCIET MARINER

Part I

It is an ancient Mariner,
And he stoppeth one of three.
"By thy long gray beard and glittering eye,
Now wherefore stopp'st thou me?

"The Bridegroom's doors are opened wide,   5
And I am next of kin,
The guests are met, the feast is set:
May'st hear the merry din."

He holds him with his skinny hand;
"There was a ship," quoth he.   10
"Hold off! unhand me, gray-beard loon!"
Eftsoons[1] his hand dropt he.

He holds him with his glittering eye —
The Wedding-Guest stood still,
And listens like a three years' child.   15
The Mariner hath his will.

The Wedding-Guest sat on a stone:
He cannot choose but hear;
And thus spake on that ancient man,
The bright-eyed Mariner.   20

"The ship was cheered, the harbor cleared,
Merrily did we drop
Below the Kirk, below the hill,
Below the light-house top.

"The sun cam up upon the left,   25
Out of the sea came he!
And he shone bright, and on the right
Went down into the sea.

"Higher and higher eevry day,
Till over the mast at noon—"   30
The Wedding-Guest here beat his breast,
For he heard the loud bassoon.

The bride hath paced into the hall,
Red as a rose is she;
Nodding their heads before her goes   35
The merry minstrelsy.

---

1. immediately

The Wedding-Guest he beat his breast,
Yet he cannot choose but hear;
And thus spake on that ancient man,
The bright-eyed Mariner.   40

"And now the Storm-blast came, and he
Was tyrannous and strong:
He struck with his o'ertaking wings,
And chased us south along.

"With sloping masts and dipping prow,   45
As who pursued with yell and blow
Still treads the shadow of his foe,
And forward bends his head,
The ship drove fast, loud roared the blast,
And southward aye we fled.   50

"And now there came both mist and snow,
And it grew wondrous cold:
And ice, mast-high, came floating by,
As green as emerald.

"And through the drifts the snowy clifts   55
Did send a dismal sheen:
Nor shapes of men nor beasts we ken —
The ice was all between.

"The ice was here, the ice was there,
The ice was all around: 60
It cracked and growled, and roared and howled,
Like noises in a swound!

"At length did cross an Albatross,
Thorough the fog it came;
As if it had been a Christian soul,   65
We hailed it in God's name.

"It ate the food it ne'er had eat,
And round and round it flew.
The ice did split with a thunder-fit;
The helsman steered us through!   70

"And a good south wind sprung up behind;
The Albatross did follow,
And every day, for food and play,
Came to the mariners' hollo!

"In mist or cloud, on mast or shroud,   75
It perched for vespers nine;
Whiles all the night, through fog-smoke white,
Glimmered the white moon-shine."

"God save thee, ancient Mariner!
From the fiends, that plague thee thus! —   80
Why look'st thou so?" — "With my crossbow
I shot the Albatross!

Part II

"The Sun now rose upon the right:
Out of the sea came he,
Still hid in mist, and on the left   85
Went down into the sea.

"And the good south wind still blew behind,
But no sweet bird did follow,
Nor any day for food or play
Came to the Mariners' hollo!   90

"And I had done a hellish thing,
And it would work 'em woe:
For all averred, I had killed the bird
That made the breeze to blow.
Ah wretch! said they, the bird to slay,   95
That made the breeze to blow!

"Nor dim nor red, like God's own head,
The glorious Sun uprist:
Then all averred, I had killed the bird
That brought the fog and mist.   100
'Twas right, said they, such birds to slay,
That bring the fog and mist.

"The fair breeze blew, the white foam flew,
The furrow followed free;
We were the first that ever burst   105
Into that silent sea.

"Down dropt the breeze, the sails dropt down,
'Twas sad as sad could be;
And we did speak only to break
The silence of the sea!   110

"All in a hot and copper sky,
The bloody Sun, at noon,
Right up above the mast did stand,
No bigger than the Moon.

"Day after day, day after day,   115
We stuck, nor breath nor motion;
As idle as a painted ship
Upon a painted ocean.

"Water, water, everywhere,
And all the boards did shrink;   120
Water, water, everywhere,
Nor any drop to drink.

"The very deep did rot: O Christ!
That ever this should be!
Yea, slimy things did crawl with legs   125
Upon the slimy sea.

"About, about, in reel and rout
The death-fires danced at night;
The water, like a witch's oils,
Burnt green, and blue and white.   130

"And some in dreams assured were
Of the Spirit that plagued us so;
Nine fathom deep he had followed us
From the land of mist and snow.

"And every tongue, through utter drought,   135
Was withered at the root;
We could not speak, no more than if
We had been chocked with soot.

"Ah! well-a-day! what evil looks
Had I from old and young!   140
Instead of the cross, the Albatross
About my neck was hung.

Part III

"There passed a weary time. Each throat
Was parched, and glazed each eye.
A weary time! a weary time!   145
How glazed each weary eye,
When looking westward, I beheld
A something in the sky.

"At first it seemed a little speck,
And then it seemed a mist;   150
It moved and moved, and took at last
A certain shape, I wist.[2]

"A speck, a mist, a shape, I wist!
And still it neared and neared:
As if it dodged a water-sprite,   155
It plunged and tacked and veered.

"With throats unslacked, with black lips baked,
We could not laugh nor wail;
Through utter drought all dumb we stood,
I bit my arm, I sucked the blood,   160
And cried, A sail; a sail!

"With throats unslaked, with black lips baked,
Agape they heard me call:
Gramercy! they for joy did grin,
And all at once their breath drew in, 165
As they were drinking all.

"See! see! (I cried) she tacks no more!
Hither to work us weal, —
Without a breeze, without a tide,
She steadies with upright keel!   170

---

2. *ywis*, certainly

"The western wave was all aflame,
The day was well nigh done!
Almost upon the western wave
Rested the broad bright Sun;
When that strange shape drove suddenly   175
Betwixt us and the Sun.

"And straight the Sun was flecked with bars,
(Heaven's Mother send us grace!)
As if through a dungeon-grate he peered
With broad and burning face.   180

"Alas! (thought I, and my heart beat loud)
How fast she nears and nears!
Are those her sails that glance in the Sun,
Like restless gossameres?

"Are those her ribs through which the Sun   185
Did peer, as through a grate?
And is that Woman all her crew?
Is that a Death? and are there two?
Is Death that woman's mate?

"Her lips were red, her looks were free,   190
Her locks were yellow as gold:
Her skin was as white as leprosy,
The Night-mare Life-in-Death was she,
Who thicks man's blood with cold.

"The naked hulk alongside came,   195
And the twain were casting dice;
'The game is done! I've won! I've won!'
Quoth she, and whistles thrice.

"The Sun's rim dips; the stars rush out: 200
At one stride comes the dark;
With far-heard whisper, o'er the sea,
Off shot the spectre-bark.

"We listened and looked sideways up!
Fear at my heart, as at a cup,
My life-blood seemed to sip!   205

The stars were dim, and thick the night,
The steersman's face by his lamp gleamed white;
From the sails the dew did drip —
Till clomb above the eastern bar
The horned Moon, with one bright star   210
Within the nether tip.

"One after one, by the star-dogged Moon,
Too quick for groan or sigh,
Each turned his face with a ghastly pang,
And cursed me with his eye.   215

"Four times fifty living men,
(And I heard nor sigh nor groan)
With heavy thump, a lifeless lump,
They dropped down one by one.

"Their souls did from their bodies fly, —   220
They fled to bliss or woe!
And every soul, it passed me by
Like the whizz of my cross-bow!"

Part IV

"I fear thee, ancient Mariner!
I fear thy skinny hand!   225
And thou art long, and lank, and brown,
As is the ribbed sea-sand.

"I fear thee and thy glittering eye,
And thy skinny hand, so brown." —
"Fear not, fear not, thou Wedding-Guest!   230
This body dropt not down.

"Alone, alone, all, all alone,
Alone on a wide, wide sea!
And never a saint took pity on
My soul in agony.   235

"The many men, so beautiful!
And they all dead did lie:
And a thousand thousand slimy things
Lived on; and so did I.

"I looked upon the rotting sea,   240
And drew my eyes away;
I looked upon the rotting deck,
And there the dead men lay.

"I looked to heaven, and tried to pray;
But or ever a prayer had gusht,   245
A wicked whisper came, and made
My heart as dry as dust.

"I closed my lids, and kept them close,
And the balls like pulses beat;
For the sky and the sea, and the sea and the sky   250
Lay like a load on my weary eye,
And the dead were at my feet.

"The cold sweat melted from their limbs,
Nor rot nor reek did they:
The look with which they looked on me   255
Had never passed away.

"An orphan's curse would drag to hell
A spirit from on high;
But oh! more horrible than that
Is a curse in a dead man's eye!   260
Seven days, seven nights, I saw that curse,
And yet I could not die.

"The moving Moon went up the sky,
And nowhere did abide:
Softly she was going up,   265
And a star or two beside—

"Her beams bemocked the sultry main,
Like April hoar-frost spread;
But where the ship's huge shadow lay,
The charmed water burnt alway   270
A still and awful red.

"Beyond the shadow of the ship,
I watched the water-snakes:
They moved in tracks of shining white,
And when they reared, the elfish light   275
Fell off in hoary flakes.

"Within the shadow of the ship
I watched their rich attire:
Blue, glossy green, and velvet black,
They coiled and swam; and every track   280
Was a flash of golden fire.

"O happy living things! no tongue
Their beauty might declare:
A spring of love gushed from my heart,
And I blessed them unaware;   285
Sure my kind saint took pity on me,
And I blessed them unaware.

"The selfsame moment I could pray;
And from my neck so free
The Albatross fell off, and sank   290
Like lead into the sea.

Part V

"Oh sleep! it is a gentle thing,
Beloved from pole to pole!
To Mary Queen the praise be given!
She sent the gentle sleep from Heaven,   295
That slid into my soul.

"The silly³ buckets on the deck,
That had so long remained,
I dreamt that they were filled with dew;
And when I awoke, it rained.   300

"My lips were wet, my throat was cold,
My garments all were dank;
Sure I had drunken in my dreams,
And still my body drank.

---

3.   empty

"I moved, and could not feel my limbs:: 305
I was so light — almost
I thought that I had died in sleep,
And was a blessed ghost.

"And soon I heard a roaring wind:
It did not come anear; 310
But with its sound it shook the sails,
That were so thin and sere.

"The upper air burst into life!
And a hundred fire-flags sheen,
To and fro they were hurried about! 315
And to and fro, and in and out,
The wan stars danced between.

"And the coming wind did roar more loud,
And the sails did sigh like sedge;
And the rain poured down from one black cloud; 320
The Moon was at its edge.

"The thick black cloud was cleft, and still
The Moon was at its side:
Like waters shot from some high crag,
The lightning fell with never a jag, 325
A river steep and wide.

"The loud wind never reached the ship,
Yet now the ship moved on!
Beneath the lightning and the Moon,
The dead men gave a groan. 330

"They groaned, they stirred, they all uprose,
Nor spake, nor moved their eyes;
It had been strange, even in a dream,
To have seen those dead men rise.

"The helmsman steered, the ship moved on; 335
Yet never a breeze up blew;
The mariners all 'gan work the ropes,
Where they were wont to do;
They raised their limbs like lifeless tools —
We were a ghastly crew. 340

"The body of my brother's son
Stood by me, knee to knee:
The body and I pulled at one rope,
But he said nought to me."

"I fear thee, Ancient Mariner!"   345
"Be calm, thou Wedding-Guest!
'Twas not those souls that fled in pain,
Which to their corses came again,
But a troop of spirits blest:

"For when it dawned — they dropped their arms,   350
And clustered round the mast;
Sweet sounds rose slowly through their mouths,
And from their bodies passed.

"Around, around, flew each sweet sound,
Then darted to the Sun;   355
Slowly the sounds came back again,
Now mixed, now one by one.

"Sometimes a-dropping from the sky
I heard the skylark sing;
Sometimes all little birds that are,   360
How they seemed to fill the sea and air
With their sweet jargoning!

"And now 'twas like all instruments,
Now like a lonely flute;
And now it is an angel's song,   365
That makes the heavens be mute.

"It ceased; yet still the sails made on
A pleasant noise till noon,
A noise like of a hidden brook
In the leafy month of June,   370
That to the sleeping woods all night
Singeth a quiet tune.

"Till noon we quietly sailed on,
Yet never a breeze did breathe:

Slowly and smoothly went the ship,   375
Moved onward from beneath.

"Under the keel nine fathom deep,
From the land of mist and snow:
The Spirit slid: and it was he
That made the ship to go.   380
The sails at noon left off their tune,
And the ship stood still also.

"The Sun, right up above the mast,
Had fixed her to the ocean:
But in a minute she 'gan stir,   385
With a short uneasy motion —
Backwards and forwards half her length
With a short uneasy motion.

"Then like a pawing horse let go,
She made a sudden bound: 390
It flung the blood into my head,
And I fell down in a swound.

"How long in that same fit I lay,
I have not to declare;
But ere my living life returned,   395
I heard, and in my soul discerned,
Two voices in the air.

" 'Is it he?' quoth one, 'Is this the man?
By him who died on cross,
With his cruel bow he laid full low   400
The harmless Albatross.

" 'The Spirit who bideth by himself
In the land of mist and snow,
He loved the bird that loved the man
Who shot him with his bow.'   405

"The other was a softer voice,
As soft as honey-dew:
Quoth he, 'The man hath penance done,
And penance more will do.' "

Part VI

First Voice
" 'But tell me, tell me! speak again,   410
Thy soft response renewing —
What makes that ship drive on so fast?
What is the ocean doing?'

Second Voice
" 'Still as a slave before his lord,
The ocean hath no blast;   415
His great bright eye most silently
Up to the Moon is cast —

" 'If he may know which way to go;
For she guides him smooth or grim.
See, brother, see! how graciously   420
She looketh down on him.'

First Voice
" 'But why drives on that ship so fast,
Without or wave or wind?'

Second Voice
" 'The air is cut away before,
And closes from behind.'   425

" 'Fly, brother, fly! more high, more high!
Or we shall be belated:
For slow and slow that ship will go,
When the Mariner's trance is abated.'

"I woke, and we were sailing on   430
As in a gentle weather:
'Twas night, calm night, the moon was high;
The dead men stood together.

"All stood together on the deck,
For a charnel-dungeon fitter: 435
All fixed on me their stony eyes,
That in the Moon did glitter.

"The pang, the curse, with which they died,
Had never passed away:
I could not draw my eyes from theirs,   440
Nor turn them up to pray.

"And now this spell was snapt: once more
I viewed the ocean green,
And looked far forth, yet little saw
Of what had else been seen.   445

"Like.one, that on a lonesome road
Doth walk in fear and dread,
And having once turned round, walks on,
And turns no more his head;
Because he knows, a frightful fiend   450
Both close behind him tread.

"But soon there breathed a wind on me,
Nor sound nor motion made:
Its path was not upon the sea,
In ripple or in shade.   455

"It raised my hair, it fanned my cheek
Like a meadow-gale of spring —
It mingled strangely with my fears,
Yet it felt like a welcoming.

"Swiftly, swiftly flew the ship,   460
Yet she sailed softly too:
Sweetly, sweetly blew the breeze
On me alone it blew.

"Oh! dream of joy! is this indeed
The light-house top I see?   465
Is this the hill? is this the kirk?
Is this mine own countree?

"We drifted o'er the harbor-bar,
And I with sobs did pray —
O let me be awake, my God!   470
Or let me sleep alway.

"The harbor-bay was clear as glass,
So smoothly it was strewn!
And on the bay the moonlight lay,
And the shadow of the Moon.   475

"The rock shone bright, the kirk no less,
That stands above the rock:
The moonlight steeped in silentness
The steady weathercock.

"And.the bay was white with silent light   480
Till, rising from the same,
Full many shapes, that shadows were,
In crimson colors came.

"A little distance from the prow
Those crimson shadows were: 485
I turned my eyes upon the deck —
Oh, Christ! what saw I there!

"Each corse lay flat, lifeless and flat,
And, by the holy rood!
A man all light, a seraph-man,   490
On every corse there stood.

"This seraph-band, each waved his hand:
It was a heavenly sight!
They stood as signals to the land,
Each one a lovely light.   495

"This seraph-band, each waved his hand,
No voice did they impart —
No voice; mut oh! the silence sank
Like music on my heart.

"But soon I heard the dash of oars,   500
I heard the Pilot's cheer;
My head was turned perforce away,
And I saw a boat appear.

"The Pilot and the Pilot's boy,
I heard them coming fast: 505

Dear Lord in Heaven! it was a joy
The dead men could not blast.

"I saw a third — I heard his voice:
It is the Hermit good!
He singeth loud his godly hymns   510
That he makes in the wood.
He'll shrieve my soul, he'll wash away
The Albatross's blood.

                    Part VII

"This Hermit good lives in that wood
Which slopes down to the sea.   515
How loudly his sweet voice he rears!
He loves to talk with marineres
That come from a far countree.

"He kneels at morn, and noon, and eve —
He hath a cushion plump: 520
It is the moss that wholly hides
The rotted old oak-stump.

"The skiff-boat neared: I heard them talk,
'Why this is strange, I throw!
Where are those lights so many and fair,   525
That signal made but now?'

" 'Strange, by my faith!' the Hermit said —
'And they answered not our cheer!
The planks looked warped! and see those sails,
How thin they are and sere!   530
I never saw aught like to them,
Unless perchance it were

" 'Brown skeletons of leaves that lag
My forest-brook along;
When the ivy-tod is heavy with snow,   535
And the owlet whoops to the wolf below,
That eats the she-wolf's young.'

" 'Dear Lord! it hath a fiendish look —
(The Pilot made reply)
I am a-feared' — 'Push on, push on!'   540
Sand the Hermit cheerily.

"The boat came closer to the ship,
But I nor spake nor stirred;
The boat came closer beneath the ship,
And straight a sound was heard.   545

"Under the water it rumbled on,
Still louder and more dread:
It reached the ship, it split the bay;
The ship went down like lead.

"Stunned by that loud and dreadful sound,   550
Which sky and ocean smote,
Like one that hath been seven days drowned
My body lay afloat;
But swift as dreams, myself I found
Within the Pilot's boat.   555

"Upon the whirl, where sank the ship,
The boat spun round and round;
And all was still, save that the hill
Was telling of the sound.

"I moved my lips — the Pilot shrieked   560
And fell down in a fit;
The holy Hermit raised his eyes,
And prayed where he did sit.

I took the oars: the Pilot's boy,
Who now doth crazy go,   565
Laughed loud and long, and all the while
His eyes went to and fro.
'Ha! ha!' quoth he, 'full plain I see,
The Devil knows how to row.'

"And now, all in my own countree,   570
I stood on the firm land!
The Hermit stepped forth from the boat,
And scarcely he could stand.

" 'O shrieve me, shrieve me, holy man!'
The Hermit crossed his brow.   575
'Say quick,' quoth he, 'I bid thee say —
What manner of man art thou?'

"Forthwith this frame of mine was wrenched
With a woeful agony,
Which forced me to begin my tale;   580
And then it left me free.

"Since then, at an uncertain hour,
That agony returns;
And till my ghastly tale is told,
This heart within me burns.   585

"I pass, like night, from land to land;
I have strange power of speech;
That moment that his face I see,
I know the man that must hear me:
To him my tale I teach.   590

"What loud uproar bursts from that door!
The wedding-guests are there:
But in the garden-bower the bride
And bride-maids singing are:
And hark the little vesper bell,   595
Which biddeth me to prayer!

"O Wedding-Guest! this soul hath been
Alone on a wide, wide sea:
So lonely 'twas, that God himself
Scarce seemed there to be.   600

"Oh sweeter than the marriage-feast,
'Tis sweeter far to me,
To walk together to the kirk
With a goodly company! —

"To walk together to the kirk,   605
And all together pray,

While each to his great Father bends,
Old men, and babes, and loving friends,
And youths and maidens gay!

"Farewell, farewell! but this I tell   610
To thee, thou Wedding-Guest!
He prayeth well, who loveth well
Both man and bird and beast.

"He prayeth best, who loveth best
All things both great and small;   615
For the dear God who loveth us,
He made and loveth all."

The Mariner, whose eye is bright,
Whose beard with age is hoar,
Is gone: and now the Wedding-Guest   620
Turned from the bridegroom's door.

He went like one that hath been stunned,
And is of sense forlon:
A sadder and a wiser man,
He rose the morrow morn.   625

GEORGE GORDON, LORD BYRON (1788-1825)

"SHE WALKS IN BEAUTY"

She walks in beauty, like the night
    Of cloudless climes and starry skies;
And all that's best of dark and bright
    Meet in her aspect and her eyes:
Thus mellowed to that tender light   5
    Which heaven to gaudy day denies.

One shade the more, one ray the less,
    Had half impaired the nameless grace
Which waves in every raven tress,
    Or softly lightens o'er the face;   10
Where thoughts serenely sweet express
    How pure, how dear their dwelling-place.

And on that cheek, and o'er that brow,
   So soft, so calm, yet eloquent,
The smiles that win, the tints that glow,   15
   But tell of days in goodness spent,
A mind at peace with all below,
   A heart whose love is innocent!

THE DESTRUCTION OF SENNACHERIB

(II Kings, XIX)

The Assyrian came down like a wolf on the fold,
And his cohorts were gleaming in purple and gold;
And the sheen of their spears was like stars on the sea,
When the blue wave rolls nightly on deep Galilee.

Like the leaves of the forest when Summer is green,   5
That host with their banners at sunset were seen:
Like the leaves of the forest when Autumn hath blown,
That host on the morrow lay withered and strown.

For the Angel of Death spread his wings on the blast,
And breathed in the face of the foe as he passed;   10
And the eyes of the sleepers waxed deadly and chill,
And their hearts but once heaved, and forever grew still!

And there lay the steed with his nostril all wide,
But through it there rolled not the breath of his pride,
And the foam of his gasping lay white on the turf,   15
And cold as the spray of the rock-beating surf.

And there lay the rider distorted and pale,
With the dew on his brow, and the rust on his mail:
And the tents were all silent — the banners alone —
The lances unlifted — the trumpet unblown.   20

And the widows of Ashur are loud in their wail,
And the idols are broke in the temple of Baal;
And the might of the Gentile, unsmote by the sword,
Hath melted like snow in the glance of the Lord!

SONNET ON CHILLON

Eternal Spirit of the chainless Mind!
  Brightest in dungeons, Liberty! thou art;
  For there thy habitation is the heart —
The heart which love of thee alone can bind,
And when thy sons to fetters are consigned —   5
  To fetters, and the damp vault's dayless gloom,
  Their country conquers with their martyrdom,
And Freedom's fame finds wings on every wind.
Chillon! thy prison is a holy place,
  And thy sad floor an altar — for 'twas trod   10
Until his very steps have left a trace
  Worn, as if thy cold pavement were a sod,
By Bonnivard![1] — May none those marks efface!
  For they appeal from tyranny to God.

FROM *CHILDE HAROLD'S PILGRIMAGE*

I have not loved the World, nor the World me;
I have not flattered its rank breath, nor bowed
To its idolatries a patient knee,
Nor coined my cheek to smiles, — nor cried aloud
In worship of an echo: in the crowd   5
They could not deem me one of such — I stood
Among them, but not of them — in a shroud
Of thoughts which were not their thoughts, and still could,
Had I not filed my mind, which thus itself subdued.

I have not loved the World, nor the World me, —   10
But let us part fair foes; I do believe,
Though I have found them not, that there may be
Words which are things, — hopes which will not deceive,
And Virtues which are merciful, nor weave
Snares for the failing: I would also deem   15
O'er others' griefs that some sincerely grieve —
That two, or one, are almost what they seem, —
That Goodness is no name — and Happiness no dream.

---

1.   16th century political prisoner at Chillon

DEDICATION TO *DON JUAN*

Bob Southey! You're a poet — Poet laureate,
   And representative of all the race;
Although 'tis true that you turned out a Tory at
   Last — yours has lately been a common case;
And now, my Epic Renegade! what are ye at?   5
   With all the Lakers, in and out of place?
A nest of tuneful persons, to my eye
Like "four and twenty Blackbirds in a pye;

"Which pye being opened they began to sing"
   (This old song and new simile holds good),   10
"A dainty dish to set before the King,"
   Or Regent, who admires such kind of food; —
And Coleridge, too, has lately taken wing,
   But like a hawk encumbered with his hood —
Explaining metaphysics to the nation —   15
I wish he would explain his Explanation.

You, Bob! are rather insolent, you know,
   At being disappointed in your wish
To supersede all warblers here below
   And be the only Blackbird in the dish;   20
And then you overstrain yourself, or so,
   And tumble downward like the flying fish
Gasping on deck, because you soar too high, Bob
And fall for lack of moisture quite-a-dry, Bob!

And Wordsworth, in a rather long "Excursion"[2]   25
   (I think the quarto holds five hundred pages),
Has given a sample from the vasty version
   Of his new system to perplex the sages;
'Tis poetry —at least by his assertion,
   And may appear so when the dog-star rages — 30
And he who understands it would be able
To add a story to the Tower of Babel!

---

2. title of a poem

You — Gentlemen! by dint of long seculsion
 From better company, have kept your own
At Keswick,[3] and through still continued fusion   35
 Of one another's minds, at last have grown
To deem as a most logical conclusion,
 That poesy has wreaths for you alone;
There is a narrowness in such a notion,
Which makes me wish you'd change your lakes for ocean. 40

I would not imitate the petty thought,
 Nor coin my self-love to so base a vice,
For all the glory your conversion brought,
 Since gold alone should not have been its price,
You have your salary; was't for that you wrought?   45
 And Wordsworth has his place in the Exise.
You're shabby fellows — true — but poets still,
And duly seated on the immortal hill.

Your bays may hide the baldness of your brows —
 Perhaps some virtuous blushes; — let them go —   50
To you I envy neither fruit nor boughs —
 And for the fame you would engross below,
The field is universal, and allows
 Scope to all such as feel the inherent glow;
Scott, Rogers, Campbell, Moore, and Crabbe[4] will try   55
'Gainst you the question with posterity.

For me, who, wandering with pedestrian Muses,
 Contend not with you on the winged steed,
I wish your fate may yield ye, when she chooses,
 The fame you envy, and the skill you need;   60
And recollect a poet nothing loses
 In giving to his brethren their full meed
Of merit, and complaint of present days
Is not the certain path to future praise.

He that reserves his laurels for posterity   65
 (Who does not often claim the bright reversion)
Has generally no great crop to spare it, he
 Being only injured by his own assertion;
And although here and there some glorious rarity

---

3. a town in the Lake Country
4. lesser poets

Arise like Titan from the sea's immersion,   70
The major part of such appellants go
To — God knows where — for no one else can know.

If, fallen in evil days on evil tongues,
    Milton appealed to the Avenger, Time,
If Time, the Avenger, execrates his wrongs,   75
    And makes the word *"Miltonic"* mean *"sublime,"*
He deigned not to belie his soul in songs,
    Nor turn his very talent to a crime;
He did not loathe the Sire to laud the Son,
But closed the tyrant-hater he begun.   80

Think'st thou, could he — the blind Old Man — arise,
    Like Samuel from the grave, to freeze once more
The blood of monarchs with his prophecies,
    Or be alive again — against all hoar
With time and trials, and those helpless eyes,   85
    And heartless daughters — worn — and pale — and poor;
Would *he* adore a sultan? *he* obey
The intellectual eunuch Castlereagh?[5]

Cold-blooded, smooth-faced, placid miscreant!
    Babbling its sleek young hands in Erin's gore   90
And thus for wider carnage taught to pant,
    Transferred to gorge upon a sister shore,
The vulgarest tool that Tyranny could want,
    With just enough of talent, and no more,
To lengthen fetters by another fixed,   95
And offer poison long already mixed.

An orator of such set trash of phrase
    Ineffably — legitimately vile,
That even its grossest flatterers dare not praise,
    Nor foes — all nations — condescend to smile;   100
Not even a sprightly blunder's spark can blaze
    From that Ixion grindstone's ceaseless toil,
That turns and turns to give the world a notion
Of endless torments and perpetual motion.

A bungler even in its disgusting trade,   105
    And botching, patching, leaving still behind

---

5. Foreign Secretary

Something of which its masters are afraid,
   States to be curbed, and thoughts to be confined,
Conspiracy or Congress to be made —
   Cobbling at manacles for all mankind —   110
A tinkering slave-maker, who mends old chains,
With God and man's abhorrence for its gains.

If we may judge of matter by the mind,
   Emasculated to the marrow, *It*
Hath but two objects, how to serve, and bind,   115
   Deeming the chain it wears even men may fit,
Eutropius of its many masters — blind
   To worth as freedom, wisdom as to wit,
Fearless — because *no* feeling dwells in ice,
Its very courage stagnates to a vice.   120

Where shall I turn me not to *view* its bonds,
   For I will never *feel* them? — Italy!
Thy late reviving Roman soul desponds
   Beneath the lie this State-thing breathed o'er thee —
Thy clanking chain, and Erin's yet green wounds,   125
   Have voices — tongues to cry aloud for me.
Europe has slaves, allies, kings, armies still,
And Southey lives to sing them very ill.

Meantime, Sir Laureate, I proceed to dedicate,
   In honest simple verse, this song to you.   130
And, if in flattering strains I do not predicate,
   'Tis that I still retain my "buff and blue";[6]
My politics as yet are all to educate:
   Apostasy's so fashionable, too,
To keep *one* creed's a task grown quite Herculean: 135
It is not so, my Tory, Ultra-Julian?

---

6. Whig colors

PERCY BYSSHE SHELLEY (1792-1822)

OZYMANDIAS

I met a traveler from an antique land,
Who said: Two vast and trunkless legs of stone
Stand in the desert. Near them, on the sand,
Half sunk, a shattered visage lies, whose frown,
And wrinkled lip, and sneer of cold command,   5
Tell that its sculptor well those passions read,
Which yet survive, stamped on these lifeless things,
The hand that mocked them and the heart that fed:
And on the pedestal these words appear:
"My name is Ozymandias, King of Kings: 10
Look on my works, ye Mighty, and despair!"
Nothing beside remains. Round the decay
Of that colossal wreck, boundless and bare
The lone and level sands stretch far away.

FINAL CHORUS FROM *HELLAS*

The world's great age begins anew,
  The golden years return,
The earth doth like a snake renew
  Her winter weeds outworn:
Heaven smiles, and faiths and empires gleam,   5
Like wrecks of a dissolving dream.

A brighter Hellas rears its mountains
  From waves serener far;
A new Peneus rolls his fountains
  Against the morning star.   10
Where fairer Tempes bloom, there sleep
Young Cyclads on a sunnier deep.

A loftier Argo cleaves the main,
  Fraught with a later prize;
Another Orpheus sings again,   15
  And loves, and weeps, and dies.
A new Ulysses leaves once more
Calypso for his native shore.

Oh! write no more the tale of Troy,
    If earth Death's scroll must be!   20
Nor mix with Laian rage the joy
    Which dawns upon the free,
Although a subtler Sphinx renew
Riddles of death Thebes never knew.

Another Athens shall arise,   25
    And to remoter time
Bequeath, like sunset to the skies,
    The splendor of its prime;
And leave, if naught so bright may live,
All earth can take or heaven can give.   30

Saturn and Love their long repose
    Shall burst, more bright and good
Than all who fell, than One who rose,
    Than many unsubdued:
Not gold, not blood, their altar dowers,   35
But votive tears and symbol flowers.

Oh, cease! must hate and death return?
    Cease! must men kill and die?
Cease! drain not to its dregs the urn
    Of bitter prophecy.   40
The world is weary of the past.
Oh, might it die or rest at last!

ODE TO THE WEST WIND

I

O wild West Wind, thou breath of Autumn's being,
Thou, from whose unseen presence the leaves dead
Are driven, like ghosts from an enchanter fleeing,

Yellow, and black, and pale, and hectic red,
Pestilence-stricken multitudes: O thou,   5
Who chariotest to their dark wintry bed

The winged seeds, where they lie cold and low,
Each like a corpse within its grave, until
Thine azure sister of the Spring shall blow

Her clarion o'er the dreaming earth, and fill   10
(Driving sweet buds like flocks to feed in air)
With living hues and odors plain and hill:

Wild Spirit, which art moving everywhere;
Destroyer and preserver; hear, oh, hear!

II

Thou on whose stream, 'mid the steep sky's commotion,   15
Loose clouds like earth's decaying leaves are shed,
Shook from the tangled boughs of Heaven and Ocean,

Angels of rain and lightning: there are spread
On the blue surface of thine aery surge,
Like the bright hair uplifted from the head   20

Of some fierce Maenad, even from the dim verge
Of the horizon to the zenith's height,
The locks of the approaching storm. Thou dirge

Of the dying year, to which this closing night
Will be the dome of a vast sepulchre,   25
Vaulted with all thy congregated might

Of vapors, from whose solid atmosphere
Black rain, and fire, and hail will burst: oh, hear!

III

Thou who didst waken from his summer dreams
The blue Mediterranean, where he lay,   30
Lulled by the coil of his crystalline streams,

Beside a pumice isle in Baiae's bay,
And saw in sleep old palaces and towers
Quivering with the wave's intenser day,

All overgrown with azure moss and flowers   35
So sweet, the sense faints picturing them! Thou
For whose path the Atlantic's level powers

Cleave themselves into chasms, while far below
The sea-blooms and the oozy woods which wear
The sapless foliage of the ocean, know   40

Thy voice, and suddenly grow gray with fear,
And tremble and despoil themselves: oh, hear!

                                IV

If I were a dead leaf thou mightest bear;
If I were a swift cloud to fly with thee;
A wave to pant beneath thy power, and share   45

The impulse of thy strength, only less free
Than thou, O uncontrollable! If even
I were as in my boyhood, and could be

The comrade of thy wanderings over Heaven,
As then, when to outstrip thy skiey speed   50
Scarce seemed a vision; I would ne'er have striven

As thus with thee in prayer in my sore need.
Oh, lift me as a wave, a leaf, a cloud!
I fall upon the thorns of life! I bleed!

A heavy weight of hours has chained and bowed   55
One too like thee: tameless, and swift, and proud.

                                V

Make me thy lyre, even as the forest is:
What if my leaves are falling like its own!
The tumult of thy mighty harmonies

Will take from both a deep, autumnal tone,   60
Sweet though in sadness. Be thou, Spirit fierce,
My spirit! Be thou me, impetuous one!

Drive my dead thoughts over the universe
Like withered leaves to quicken a new birth!
And, by the incantation of this verse,   65

Scatter, as from an unextinguished hearth
Ashes and sparks, my words among mankind!
Be through my lips to unawakened earth

The trumpet of a prophecy! O Wind,
If Winter comes, can Spring be far behind?   70

JOHN KEATS (1795-1821)

FROM *ENDYMION*

A thing of beauty is a joy for ever:
Its loveliness increases; it will never
Pass into nothingness; but still will keep
A bower quiet for us, and a sleep
Full of sweet dreams, and health, and quiet breathing.   5
Therefore, on every morrow, are we wreathing
A flowery band to bind us to the earth,
Spite of despondence, of the inhuman dearth
Of noble natures, of the gloomy days,
Of all the unhealthy and o'er-darkened ways   10
Made for our searching: yes, in spite of all,
Some shape of beauty moves away the pall
From our dark spirits. Such the sun, the moon,
Trees old and young, sprouting a shady boon
For simple sheep; and such are daffodils   15
With the green world they live in; and clear rills
That for themselves a cooling covert make
'Gainst the hot season; the mid-forest brake,
Rich with a sprinkling of fair musk-rose blooms:
And such too is the grandeur of the dooms   20
We have imagined for the mighty dead;
All lovely tales that we have heard or read:
An endless fountain of immortal drink,
Pouring unto us from the heaven's brink.

LA BELLE DAME SANS MERCI

Ah, what can ail thee, wretched wight,
    Alone and palely loitering?
The sedge is withered from the lake,
    And no birds sing.

Ah, what can ail thee, wretched wight,   5
    So haggard and so woe-begone?
The squirrel's granary is full,
    And the harvest's done.

I see a lily on thy brow
    With anguish moist and fever dew,   10
And on thy cheek a fading rose
    Fast withereth too.

I met a lady in the meads,
    Full beautiful, a faery's child:
Her hair was long, her foot was light,   15
    And her eyes were wild.

I set her on my pacing steed,
    And nothing else saw all day long;
For sideways would she lean, and sing
    A faery's song.   20

I made a garland for her head,
    And bracelets too, and fragrant zone;
She looked at me as she did love,
    And made sweet moan.

She found me roots of relish sweet,   25
    And honey wild, and manna dew,
And sure in language strange she said,
    "I love thee true!"

She took me to her elfin grot,
    And there she gazed and sighed deep,   30
And there I shut her wild, sad eyes —
    So kissed to sleep.

And there we slumbered on the moss,
    And there I dreamed, ah! woe betide,
The latest dream I ever dreamed   35
    On the cold hill side.

I saw pale kings, and princes too,
    Pale warriors, death-pale were they all;
Who cried — "La belle Dame sans merci
    Hath thee in thrall!"   40

I saw their starved lips in the gloam,
    With horrid warning gaped wide,
And I awoke and found me here,
    On the cold hill side.

And this is why I sojurn here,   45
    Alone and palely loitering,
Though the sedge is withered from the lake,
    And no birds sing.

ON FIRST LOOKING INTO CHAPMAN'S HOMER

Much have I travelled in the realms of gold,
    And many goodly states and kingdoms seen;
    Round many western islands have I been
Which bards in fealty to Apollo hold.
Oft of one wide expanse had I been told,   5
    That deep-browed Homer ruled as his demesne:
    Yet did I never breathe its pure serene
Till I heard Chapman speak out loud and bold:
Then felt I like some watcher of the skies
    When a new planet swims into his ken;   10
Or like stout Cortez when with eagle eyes
    He stared at the Pacific — and all his men
Looked at each other with a wild surmise —
    Silent, upon a peak in Darien.

ODE ON A GRECIAN URN

Thou still unravished bride of quietness,
   Thou foster-child of silence and slow time,
Sylvan historian, who canst thus express
   A flowery tale more sweetly than our rhyme:
What leaf-fringed legend haunts about thy shape   5
   Of deities or mortals, or of both,
      In Tempe or the dales of Arcady?
   What man or gods are these? What maidens loth?
What mad pursuit? What struggle to escape?
   What pipes and timbrels? What wild ecstasy?   10

Heard melodies are sweet, but those unheard
   Are sweeter; therefore, ye soft pipes, play on;
Not to the sensual ear, but, more endeared,
   Pipe to the spirit ditties of no tone:
Fair youth, beneath the trees, thou canst not leave   15
   Thy song, nor ever can those trees be bare;
      Bold Lover, never, never canst thou kiss,
Though winning near the goal — yet, do not grieve;
      She cannot fade, though thou hast not thy bliss,
   For ever wilt thou love, and she be fair!   20

Ah, happy, happy boughs! that cannot shed
   Your leaves, nor ever bid the Spring adieu;
And, happy melodist, unwearied,
   For ever piping songs for ever new;
More happy love! more happy, happy love!   25
   For ever warm and still to be enjoyed,
      For ever panting and for ever young;
All breathing human passion far above,
   That leaves a heart high-sorrowful and cloyed,
      A burning forehead, and a parching tongue.   30

Who are these coming to the sacrifice?
   To what green altar, O mysterious priest,
Lead'st thou that heifer lowing at the skies,
   And all her silken flanks with garlands drest?
What little town by river or sea-shore,   35

Or mountain-built with peaceful citadel,
    Is emptied of its folk, this pious morn?
And, little town, thy streets for evermore
    Will silent be; and not a soul to tell
      Why thou are desolate, can e'er return.   40

O Attic shape! Fair attitude! with brede[1]
    Of marble men and maidens overwrought,
With forest branches and the trodden weed;
    Thou, silent form, dost tease us out of thought
As doth eternity: Cold Pastoral!   45
    When old age shall this generation waste,
      Thou shalt remain, in midst of other woe
    Than ours, a friend to man, to whom thou say'st,
"Beauty is truth, truth beauty, — that is all
    Ye know on earth, and all ye need to know."

RALPH WALDO EMERSON (1803-1882)

BRAHMA

If the red slayer think he slays,
    Or if the slain think he is slain,
They know not well the subtle ways
    I keep, and pass, and turn again.

Far or forget to me is near;   5
    Shadow and sunlight are the same;
The vanished gods to me appear;
    And one to me are shame and fame.

They reckon ill who leave me out;
    When me they fly, I am the wings;   10
I am the doubter and the doubt,
    And I the hymn the Brahmin sings.

The strong gods pine for my abode,
    And pine in vain the sacred Seven;
But thou, meek lover of the good!   15
    Find me, and turn thy back on heaven.

---

1. figured pattern

DAYS

Daughters of Time, the hypocritic Days,
Muffled and dumb like barefoot dervishes,
And marching single in an endless file,
Bring diadems and fagots in their hands.
To each they offer gifts after his will,　　　　5
Bread, kingdoms, stars, and the sky that holds them all.
I, in my pleached garden, watched the pomp,
Forgot my morning wishes, hastily
Took a few herbs and apples, and the Day
Turned and departed silent. I, too late,　　　　10
Under her solemn fillet saw the scorn.

FORBEARANCE

Hast thou named all the birds without a gun?
Loved the wood-rose, and left it on its stalk?
At rich men's tables eaten bread and pulse?
Unarmed, faced danger with a heart of trust?
And loved so well a high behavior,　　　　5
In man or maid, that thou from speech refrained,
Nobility more nobly to repay? —
O, be my friend, and teach me to be thine!

EDGAR ALLAN POE (1809-1849)

TO HELEN

Helen, thy beauty is to me
　　Like those Nicéan barks of yore,
That gently, o'er a perfumed sea,
　　The weary, way-worn wanderer bore
　　To his own native shore.　　　　5

On desperate seas long wont to roam,
　　Thy hyacinth hair, thy classic face,
Thy Naiad airs have brought me home
　　To the glory that was Greece,
　　And the grandeur that was Rome.　　　　10

Lo! in yon brilliant window-niche
　　How statue-like I see thee stand,
The agate lamp within thy hand!
　　Ah, Psyche, from the regions which
　　Are Holy-Land!

THE CITY IN THE SEA

Lo! Death hath reared himself a throne
In a strange city lying alone
Far sown within the dim West,
Where the good and the bad and the worst and the best
Have gone to their eternal rest.　　　　　　　　　　5
There shrines and palaces and towers
(Time-eaten towers that tremble not!)
Resemble nothing that is ours.
Around, by lifting winds forgot,
Resignedly beneath the sky　　　　　　　　　　　　10
The melancholy waters lie.

No rays from the holy heaven come down
On the long night-time of that town;
But light from out the lurid sea
Streams up the turrets silently —　　　　　　　　　15
Gleams up the pinnacles far and free —
Up domes — up spires — up kingly halls —
Up fanes — up Babylon-like walls —
Up shadowy long-forgotten bowers
O sculptured ivy and stone flowers —　　　　　　　20
Up many and many a marvelous shrine
Whose wreathed friezes intertwine
The viol, the violet, and the vine.

Resignedly beneath the sky
The melancholy waters lie.　　　　　　　　　　　　25
So blend the turrets and shadows there
That all seem pendulous in air,
While from a proud tower in the town
Death looks gigantically down.

There open fanes and gaping graves   30
Yawn level with the luminous waves;
But not the riches there that lie
In each idol's diamond eye—
Not the gaily-jeweled dead
Tempt the waters from their bed;   35
For no ripples curl, alas!
Along that wilderness of glass —
No swellings tell that winds may be
Upon some far-off happier sea —
No heavings hint that winds have been   40
On seas less hideously serene.

But lo, a stir is in the air!
The wave — there is a movement there!
As if the towers had thrust aside,
In slightly sinking, the dull tide —   45
As if their tops had feebly given
A void within the filmy Heaven.

The waves have now a redder glow —
The hours are breathing faint and low —
And when, amid no earthly moans,   50
Down, down that town shall settle hence,
Hell, rising from a thousand thrones,
Shall do it reverence.

IX

THE MID-NINETEENTH CENTURY

If sweeping generalizations are dangerous at all times, they become increasingly so as we approach our own time. One problem is that of perspective; it is harder to see a scene clearly when one is almost a part of it than it is to see one neatly framed by hundreds of years of history. A related problem is evaluation; a given era is not always the best judge of its own writers, and the age immediately following tends to reverse reputations. After an appreciable time, however, positions become secure: Milton, for example, may not be to the taste of the mid-twentieth century, but no critic would today suggest that he was anything but a great poet. About the major figures of one hundred years ago, however, there still is difference of opinion.

Yet another problem is the increasing size of the English-speaking world. To the British, this was the era of Victoria, but one cannot literally call American poets "Victorian." Yet by 1900 there were far more English-speaking Americans than British — to say nothing of hosts of Canadians, Australians, and even Indians and Burmese. If it is difficult to assess and pigeon-hole the British, it is well nigh impossible to make meaningful generalizations that will involve the poets of both Britain and America.

Still, a few tentative statements can be made. The Romantic Movement was an intense period; and tension can last for only so long. In England the cause that enlisted liberals of many varieties was (as has been said) reform of the suffrage. In 1832 the Reform Bill was passed. While it certainly didn't permit every Englishman to vote, it did greatly reduce the property requirement; and, more important, it changed election districts to abolish the rotten boroughs: Parliament was now approximately proportional to population.

The Reform Bill did not reform as much as its backers had hoped — or conservatives had feared. It took power increasingly away from the country gentry and gave it increasingly to the factory owners; the change was "liberal" only if one carefully defines the term. And so a note of disillusion was added to the quite natural let-down when the great cause seemed won; this combination of disillusion and release of tension can be marked in Victorian poetry.

In the United States the great cause was Abolition — and the great moment came in 1865. Romanticism can probably be said to have lasted until the Civil War; the "American Victorians" seem to come on the scene rather later than their British counterparts.

As the century progressed, at least three sets of ideas tended to accentuate the pessimism of the time. Each was disillusioning because it seemed to de-humanize man. The first such set was turned loose by Karl Marx; it found expression in the "Communist Manifesto" of 1848. One of Marx's main points was *economic determinism* — the notion that a man's economic status determines his conduct in all situations. Marx probably carried this doctrine to excess; some of his followers certainly did. Taken with caution, it is useful: the student of American History should know that the framers of the United States Constitution were almost to a man conservative and wealthy, and that they viewed their work (among other things) as a bulwark against radicalism. Useful or not, however, economic determinism did make men appear to be less free, less responsible — a little closer to Pavlov's dogs.

Of far wider significance in the English-speaking world were the ideas of Charles Darwin; *The Origin of the Species* was published in 1859. There were so many nonsensical arguments over Darwinism that the actually rather mild things Darwin really said are sometimes forgotten. What was discouraging to many people — perhaps particularly poets — was not the fact that the world apparently had not been created in 4004 B.C.; as a matter of fact, for quite some time it had been realized that the Biblical record, treated as science, needed a certain amount of "interpretation." What *was* discouraging was man's loss of his special place in the universe. If he was but one step removed from the apes, he was obviously far from the angels.

More de-humanizing than either Marxism or Darwinism, because far more universally accepted, was the economic theory that dominated English and American thinking. Called *laissez faire,* it implied that there was an economic "law" called the "law of supply and demand"; this law automatcially set prices and wages, and governments that would try to control the former or raise the latter did so at the peril of wrecking the whole economic machine. The de-humanizing aspect of this notion lay in the practice of treating "labor" strictly as a "cost" — a factor in production not fundamentally different from power or raw materials. The manager obviously bought coal at the lowest price possible, and he did the same with man and women (and children). Hence, not only were factory conditions deplorable, but attempts to improve them were branded "unscientific."

If we regard these discouraging aspects of nineteenth century life, it is difficult to see how the Victorian era should have acquired its image of boundless (and tasteless) optimism, coupled with a rather hypocritical narrowness of morality. Several factors account for the apparent contradiction. For one thing, *laissez faire* economics *did* produce vast wealth; it looked tremendous on a graph. The wealth may have been very unequally distributed, but by the second half of the century some of it was trickling down to the workers. Perhaps they lived in squalor, but they had "things" they could call their own — more such things than men had had before. And so a certain materialist optimism could be explained.

Secondly, there were both growing literacy and lowered costs of printing. As a result, there was a large body of popular literature which catered to the barely literate. Such writing did not concern itself with troubled thoughts about man's place in the universe. Ironically, the poets whom we will study did not profit from the increased literacy; indeed, the role of the poet steadily declined in influence. Education, then, another great liberal cause, seemed only to release the partially educated into a world of "progress," while the more fully educated had another reason to feel gloomy.

The narrowness of Victorian morality was certainly due in some part to Queen Victoria. She reigned from 1837 till 1901, exercising increasingly greater influence on popular taste and manners as she became more and more a fixture — and she didn't exactly become more liberal with age. Probably more important than the Queen, however, was the fact that capitalism was pushing into high place many people unused to it. When one suddenly rises to great heights, especially by rather raw means, he is perhaps likely to become as respectable as he can as fast as he can. Excessive propriety, mingled with atrocious taste, can easily result.

There were three major British Victorian poets. Alfred Tennyson, who at his best sounds like Keats, wrote a great many thoughtful poems indicating his perplexity with and concern for his age. A clergyman' son, with a traditional gentleman's education, he suffered a great personal grief in the death of a college friend, Arthur Hallam, who had been engaged to the poet's sister. This personal sorrow, plus his awareness of disturbing change in his world, colored much of his poetry with melancholy. Though he never really resolved his doubts, Tennyson's eventual mood might be called hopeful skepticism.

Tennyson became Poet Laureate at Wordsworth's death. His most popular poems in his own time were various patriotic pieces stemming from this position. Compared with most Poets Laureate, Tennyson did well, but his best verse is his more "private" writing.

Similar to Tennyson in tone, but gloomier, was Matthew Arnold. Son of a great "public school" headmaster, and a fine classical scholar, he suggests in his poetry despair with the world. This despair did not keep Arnold from serving his country well as a public official helping to establish public schools (in the American sense).

Very different was Robert Browning, the male partner in one of the more spectacular elopements of the time. His poetry is difficult — abounding in strange rhythms and highly condensed ideas. He is hard to identify with his age, though a fascination with the odd workings of the human mind might seem rather typical. His most characteristic poems are *dramatic monologues* — little plays where one actor does all the talking, and usually ends up telling more about himself than about others.

The period of Tennyson, Arnold, and Browning was also the period of America's first great poet, Walt Whitman. He belongs to the period only because of his dates, however; his content is basically Romantic, while in techniques he could be called the first of the "moderns," in which capacity he will be discussed later.

Also of this period was another American, Emily Dickinson. Her poems are unique, belonging to no school or tradition — not surprisingly, as their writer was a very quiet and retiring maiden lady. Extremely simple and apparently artless on first sight, Emily Dickinson's poems grow on the reader. Their artlessness turns out to be high art, and their simplicity becomes profound. Her range of subjects may be limited, but few poets go so deeply into them.

ALFRED, LORD TENNYSON (1809-1892)

ULYSSES

It little profits that an idle king,
By this still hearth, among these barren crags,
Matched with an aged wife, I mete and dole
Unequal laws unto a savage race,
That hoard, and sleep, and feed, and know not me.   5
I cannot rest from travel: I will drink
Life to the lees: all times I have enjoyed
Greatly, have suffered greatly, both with those
That loved me, and alone; on shore, and when
Through scudding drifts the rainy Hyades   10
Vext the dim sea. I am become a name;
For always roaming with a hungry heart
Much have I seen and known: cities of men
And manners, climates, councils, governments,
Myself not least, but honored of them all,—   15
And drunk delight of battle with my peers,
Far on the ringing plains of windy Troy.
I am a part of all that I have met;
Yet all experience is an arch wherethrough
Gleams that untraveled world, whose margin fades   20
For ever and for ever when I move.
How dull it is to pause, to make an end,
To rust unburnished, not to shine in use!
As though to breathe were life. Life piled on life
Were all too little, and of one to me   25
Little remains: but every hour is saved
From that eternal silence, something more,
A bringer of new things; and vile it were
For some three suns to store and hoard myself,
And this gray spirit yearning in desire   30
To follow knowledge, like a sinking star,
Beyond the utmost bound of human thought.

   This is my son, mine own Telemachus,
To whom I leave the scepter and the isle —
Well-loved of me, discerning to fulfill   35
This labor, by slow prudence to make mild

A rugged people, and through soft degrees
Subdue them to the useful and the good.
Most blameless is he, centered in the sphere
Of common duties, decent not to fail   40
In offices of tenderness, and pay
Meet adoration to my household gods,
When I am gone. He works his work, I mine.

    There lies the port: the vessel puffs her sail:
There gloom the dark broad seas. My mariners,   45
Souls that have toiled, and wrought, and thought with me —
That ever with a frolic welcome took
The thunder and the sunshine, and opposed
Free hearts, free foreheads — you and I are old;
Old age hath yet his honor and his toil;   50
Death closes all: but something ere the end,
Some work of noble note, may yet be done,
Not unbecoming men that strove with Gods.
The lights begin to twinkle from the rocks:
The long day wanes: the slow moon climbs: the deep   55
Moans round with many voices. Come, my friends,
'Tis not too late to seek a newer world.
Push off, and sitting well in order smite
The sounding furrows; for my purpose holds
To sail beyond the sunset, and the baths   60
Of all the western stars, until I die.
It may be that the gulfs will wash us down:
It may be we shall touch the Happy Isles,
And see the great Achilles, whom we knew.
Though much is taken, much abides; and though   65
We are not now the strength which in old days
Moved earth and heaven, that which we are, we are, —
One equal temper of heroic hearts,
Made weak by time and fate, but strong in will
To strive, to seek, to find, and not to yield.   70

FROM *IN MEMORIAM A.H.H.*[1]

LIV

O, yet we trust that somehow good
    Will be the final goal of ill,
    To pangs of nature, sins of will,
Defects of doubt, and taints of blood;

That nothing walks with aimless feet;   5
    That not one life shall be destroyed,
    Or cast as rubbish to the void,
When God hath made the pile complete;

That not a worm is cloven in vain;
    That not a moth with vain desire   10
    Is shriveled in a fruitless fire,
Or but subserves another's gain.

Behold, we know not anything;
    I can but trust that good shall fall
    At last — far off — at last, to all,   15
And every winter change to spring.

So runs my dream; but what am I?
    An infant crying in the night;
    An infant crying for the light,
And with no language but a cry.   20

LV

The wish, that of the living whole
    No life may fail beyond the grave,
    Derives it not from what we have
The likest God within the soul?

Are God and Nature then at strife,   25
    That Nature lends such evil dreams?
    So careful of the type she seems,
So careless of the single life,

---

1. Arthur Henry Hallam

That I, considering everywhere
    Her secret meaning in her deeds,   30
    And finding that of fifty seeds
She often brings but one to bear,

I falter when I firmly trod,
    And falling with my weight of cares
    Upon the great world's altar-stairs   30
That slope thro' darkness up to God,

I stretch lame hands of faith, and grope,
    And gather dust and chaff, and call
    To what I feel is Lord of all,
And faintly trust the larger hope.   40

LVI

"So careful of the type?" but no.
    From scarped cliff and quarried stone
    She cries, "A thousand types are gone;
I care for nothing, all shall go.

"Thou makest thine appeal to me.   45
    I bring to life, I bring to death;
    The spirit does but mean the breath.
I know no more." And he, shall he,

Man, her last work, who seemed so fair,
    Such splendid purpose in his eyes,   50
    Who rolled the psalm to wintry skies,
Who built him fanes of fruitless prayer,

Who trusted God was love indeed
    And love Creation's final law —
    Though Nature, red in tooth and claw   55
With ravine, shieked against his creed —

Who loved, who suffered countless ills,
    Who battled for the True, the Just,
    Be blown about the desert dust,
Or sealed within the iron hills?   60

No more? A monster then, a dream,
    A discord. Dragons of the prime,
    That tare each other in their slime,
Were mellow music matched with him.

O life as futile, then, as frail!   65
    O for thy[2] voice to soothe and bless!
    What hope of answer, or redress?
Behind the veil, behind the veil.

FROM *MORTE D'ARTHUR*

[King Arthur, dying of wounds received in his last battle, tells his sole remaining Knight of the Round Table, Sir Bedivere, to carry the magic sword, Excalibur, to a nearby lake, hurl it into the water, and bring back word of what he saw. Twice Sir Bedivere disobeys; the sword is too wonderful to part with. He is given a third and final chance; this time he throws the sword.]

Then spoke King Arthur, drawing thicker breath:
"Now see I by thine eyes that this is done.
Speak out: what is it thou hast heard, or seen?"

And answer made the bold Sir Bedivere:
"Sir King, I closed mine eyelids, lest the gems   5
Should blind my purpose, for I never saw,
Nor shall see, here or elsewhere, till I die,
Not though I live three lives of mortal men,
So great a miracle as yonder hilt.
Then with both hands I flung him, wheeling him;   10
But when I looked again, behold an arm,
Clothed in white samite, mystic, wonderful,
That caught him by the hilt, and brandished him
Three times, and drew him under in the mere."

---

2. Hallam's

And answer made King Arthur, breathing hard: 15
"My end draws nigh; 'tis time that I were gone.
Make broad thy shoulders to receive my weight,
And bear me to the margin; yet I fear
My wound hath taken cold, and I shall die."

So saying, from the pavement he half rose,   20
Slowly, with pain, reclining on his arm,
And looking wistfully with wide blue eyes
As in a picture. Him Sir Bedivere
Remorsefully regarded through his tears,
And would have spoken, but he found not words,   25
Then took with care, and kneeling on one knee,
O'er both this shoulders drew the languid hands,
And rising bore him through the place of tombs.

But, as he walked, King Arthur panted hard,
Like one that feels a nightmare on his bed   30
When all the house is mute. So sighed the King,
Muttering and murmuring at his ear, "Quick, quick!
I fear it is too late, and I shall die."
But the other swiftly strode from ridge to ridge,
Clothed with his breath, and looking, as he walked,   35
Larger than human on the frozen hills.
He heard the deep behind him, and a cry
Before. His own thought drove him like a goad.
Dry clashed his harness in the icy caves
And barren chasms, and all to left and right   40
The bare black cliff clanged round him, as he based
His feet on juts of slippery crag that rang
Sharp-smiten with the dint of armed heels —
And on a sudden, lo! the level lake,
And the long glories of the winter moon.   45

Then saw they how there hove a dusky barge,
Dark as a funeral scarf from stem to stern,
Beneath them; and descending they were ware
That all the decks were dense with stately forms
Black-stoled, black-hooded, like a dream — by these   50
Three queens with crowns of gold — and from them rose
A cry that shivered to the tingling stars,

And, as it were one voice, an agony
Of lamentation, like a wind, that shrills
All night in a waste land, where no one comes,   55
Or hath come, since the making of the world.

   Then murmured Arthur, "Place me in the barge,"
And to the barge they came. There those three queens
Put forth their hands, and took the king, and wept.
But she, that rose the tallest of them all   60
And fairest, laid his head upon her lap,
And loosed the shattered casque, and chafed his hands,
And called him by his name, complaining loud,
And dropping bitter tears against his brow
Striped with dark blood: for all his face was white   65
And colorless, and like the withered moon
Smote by the fresh beam of the springing east;
And all his greaves and cuisses dashed with drops
Of onset; and the light and lustrous curls —
That made his forehead like a rising sun   70
High from the dais-throne — were parched with dust:
Or, clotted into points and hanging loose,
Mixed with the knightly growth that fringed his lips.
So like a shattered column lay the king;
Not like that Arthur who, with lance in rest,   75
From spur to plume a star of tournament,
Shot through the lists at Camelot, and charged
Before the eyes of ladies and of kings.

   Then loudly cried the bold Sir Bedivere,
"Ah! my Lord Arthur, whither shall I go?   80
Where shall I hide my forehead and my eyes?
For now I see the true old times are dead,
When every morning brought a noble chance,
And every chance brought out a noble knight.
Such times have not been since the light that led   85
The holy Elders with the gift of myrrh.
But now the whole ROUND TABLE is dissolved
Which was an image of the mighty world;
And I, the last, go forth companionless,
And the days darken round me, and the years,   90
Among new men, strange faces, other minds."

And slowly answered Arthur from the barge:
"The old order changeth, yielding place to new,
And God fulfills Himself in many ways,
Lest one good custom should corrupt the world.   95
Comfort thyself: what comfort is in me?
I have lived my life, and that which I have done
May He within Himself make pure! but thou,
If thou shouldst never see my face again,
Pray for my soul. More things are wrought by prayer   100
That this world dreams of. Wherefore, let thy voice
Rise like a fountain for me night and day.
For what are men better than sheep or goats
That nourish a blind life within the brain,
If, knowing God, they lift not hands in prayer   105
Both for themselves and those who call them friend?
For so the whole round earth is every way
Bound by gold chains about the feet of God.
But now farewell. I am going a long way
With those thou seëst — if indeed I go —   110
(For all my mind is clouded with a doubt)
To the island-valley of Avilion;
Where falls not hail, or rain, or any snow,
Nor ever wind blows loudly, but it lies
Deep-meadowed, happy, fair with orchard-lawns   115
And bowery hollows crowned with summer sea,
Where I will heal me of my grievous wound."

So said he, and the barge with oar and sail
Moved from the brink, like some full-breasted swan
That, fluting a wild carol ere her death,   120
Ruffles her pure cold plume, and takes the flood
With swarthy webs. Long stood Sir Bedivere
Revolving many memories, till the hull
Looked one black dot against the verge of dawn,
And on the mere the wailing died away.   125

CROSSING THE BAR

Sunset and evening star,
    And one clear call for me!
And may there be no moaning of the bar,
    When I put out to sea,

But such a tide as moving seems asleep,   5
    Too full for sound and foam,
When that which drew from out the boundless deep
    Turns again home.

Twilight and evening bell,
    And after that the dark!   10
And may there be no sadness of farewell,
    When I embark;

For though from out our bourne of Time and Place
    The flood may bear me far,
I hope to see my Pilot face to face   15
    When I have crossed the bar.

ROBERT BROWNING (1812-1889)

MY LAST DUCHESS
Scene: Ferrara

That's my last Duchess painted on the wall,
Looking as if she were alive. I call
That piece a wonder, now: Frà Pandolf's hands
Worked busily a day, and there she stands.
Will't please you sit and ook at her? I said
"Frà Pandolf" by design, for never read
Strangers like you that pictured countenance,
The depth and passion of its earnest glance,
But to myself they turned (since none puts by
The curtain I have drawn for you, but I)   10
And seemed as they would ask me, if they durst,
How such a glance came there; so, not the first
Are you to turn and ask thus. Sir, 'twas not
Her husband's presence only, called that spot
Of joy into the Duchess' cheek: perhaps   15
Frà Pandolf chanced to say, "Her mantle laps
Over my Lady's wrist too much," or "Paint
Must never hope to reproduce the faint
Half-flush that dies along her throat"; such stuff

Was courtesy, she thought, and cause enough   20
For calling up that spot of joy. She had
A heart — how shall I say? — too soon made glad,
Too easily impressed; she liked whate'er
She looked on, and her looks went everywhere.
Sir, 'twas all one! My favor at her breast,   25
The dropping of the daylight in the West,
The bough of cherries some officious fool
Broke in the orchard for her, the white mule
She rode with round the terrace — all and each
Would draw from her alike the approving speech,   30
Or blush, at least. She thanked men, — good; but thanked
Somehow — I know not how — as if she ranked
My gift of a nine-hundred-years'-old name
With anybody's gift. Who'd stoop to blame
This sort of trifling? Even had you skill   35
In speech — (which I have not) — to make your will
Quite clear to such an one, and say, "Just this
Or that in you disgusts me; here you miss,
Or there exceed the mark" — and if she let
Herself be lessoned so, nor plainly set   40
Her wits to yours, forsooth, and made excuse,
— E'en then would be some stooping, and I choose
Never to stoop, Oh, sir, she smiled, no doubt,
Whene'er I passed her; but who passed without
Much the same smile? This grew; I gave commands;   45
Then all smiles stopped together. There she stands
As if alive. Will'st please you rise? We'll meet
The company below, then. I repeat,
The Count your master's known munificence
Is ample warrant that no just pretence   50
Of mine for dowry will be disallowed;
Though his fair daughter's self, as I avowed
At starting, is my object. Nay, we'll go
Together down, sir! Notice Neptune, though,
Taming a sea-horse, thought a rarity,   55
Which Claus of Innsbruck cast in bronze for me!

PROSPICE

Fear death? — to feel the fog in my throat,
  The mist in my face,
When the snows begin, and the blasts denote
  I am nearing the place,
The power of the night, the press of the storm,   5
  The post of the foe;
Where he stands, the Arch Fear in a visible form,
  Yet the strong man must go:
For the journey is done and the summit attained,
  And the barriers fall,   10
Though a battle's to fight ere the guerdon be gained,
  The reward of it all.
I was ever a fighter, so — one fight more,
  The best and the last!
I would hate that death bandaged my eyes, and forbore,   15
  And bade me creep past.
No! let me taste the whole of it, fare like my peers
  The heroes of old,
Bear the brunt, in a minute pay glad life's arrears
  Of pain, darkness and cold.   20
For sudden the worst turns the best to the brave,
  The black minute's at end,
And the elements' rage, the fiend-voices that rave,
  Shall dwindle, shall blend,
Shall change, shall become first a peace out of pain,   25
  Then a light, then thy breast,
O thou soul of my soul! I shall clasp thee again,
  And with God be the rest!

THE BISHOP ORDERS HIS TOMB AT PRAXED'S CHURCH

Rome, 15——

Vanity, saith the preacher, vanity!
Draw round my bed: is Anselm keeping back?
Nephews — sons mine . . . ah God, I know not! Well —
She, men would have to be your mother once,
Old Gandolf envied me, so fair she was!   5

What's done is done, and she is dead beside,
Dead long ago, and I am Bishop since,
And as she died so must we die ourselves,
And thence ye may perceive the world's a dream.
Life, how and what is it? As here I lie   10
In this state-chamber, dying by degrees,
Hours and long hours in the dead night, I ask,
"Do I live, am I dead?" Peace, peace seems all.
Saint Praxed's ever was the church for peace;
And so, about this tomb of mine. I fought   15
With tooth and nail to save my niche, ye know:
— Old Gandolf cozened me, despite my care;
Shrewd was that snatch from out the corner South
He graced his carrion with. God curse the same!
Yet still my niche is not so cramped but thence   20
One sees the pulpit o' the epistle-side,
And somewhat of the choir, those silent seats,
And up into the aery dome where live
The angels, and a sunbeam's sure to lurk:
And I shall find my slab of basalt there,   25
And 'neath my tabernacle take my rest,
With those nine columns round me, two and two,
The odd one at my feet where Anselm stands:
Peach-blossom marble all, the rare, the ripe

As fresh-poured red wine of a mighty pulse.   30
— Old Gandolf with his paltry onion-stone,
Put me where I may look at him! True peach,
Rosy and flawless: how I earned the prize!
Draw close: that conflagration of my church
— What then? So much was saved if aught were missed!   35
My sons, ye would not be my death? Go dig
The white-grape vineyard where the oil-press stood,
Drop water gently till the surface sink,
And if ye find .. Ah God, I know not, I! ...

Bedded in store of rotten fig-leaves soft,   40
And corded up in a tight olive-frail,
Some lump, ah God, of *lapis lazuli*,
Big as a Jew's head cut off at the nape,
Blue as a vein o'er the Madonna's breast ...

Sons, all have I bequeathed you, villas, all,   45
That brave Frascati villa with its bath,
So, let the blue lump poise between my knees,

Like God the Father's globe on both his hands
Ye worship in the Jesu Church so gay,
For Gandolf shall not choose but see and burst!   50
Swift as a weaver's shuttle fleet our years:
Man goeth to the grave, and where is he?
Did I say basalt for my slab, sons? Black —
'Twas ever antique-black I meant! How else
Shall ye contrast my frieze to come beneath?   55
The bas-relief in bronze ye promised me,
Those Pans and Nymphs ye wot of, and perchance
Some tripod, thyrsus, with a vase or so,
The Savior at his sermon on the mount,
Saint Praxed in a glory, and one Pan   60
Ready to twitch the Nymph's last garment off,
And Moses with the tables . . . but I know
Ye mark me not! What do they whisper thee,
Child of my bowels, Anselm? Ah, ye hope
To revel down my Villas while I gasp   65
Bricked o'er with beggar's moldy travertine
Which Gandolf from his tomb-top chuckles at!
Nay, boys, ye love me — all of jasper, then!
'Tis jasper ye stand pledged to, lest I grieve
My bath must needs be left behind, alas!   70
One block, pure green as a pistachio-nut,
There's plenty jasper somewhere in the world —
And have I not Saint Praxed's ear to pray
Horses for ye, and brown Greek manuscripts,
And mistresses with great smooth marbly limbs?   75
— That's if ye carve my epitaph aright,
Choice Latin, picked phrase, Tully's[1] every word,
No gaudy ware like Gandolf's second line —
Tully, my masters? Ulpian[2] serves his need!
And then how I shall lie through centuries,   80
And hear the blessed mutter of the mass,
And see God made and eaten all day long,
And feel the steady candle-flame, and taste
Good, strong, thick, stupifying incense-smoke!
For as I lie here, hours of the dead night,   85
Dying in state and by such slow degrees,

---

1. Cicero's
2. a later Latin writer

I fold my arms as if they clasped a crook,
And stretch my feet forth straight as stone can point,
And let the bedclothes, for a mortarcloth, drop
Into great laps and folds of sculptor's-work: 90
And as yon tapers dwindle, and strange thoughts
Grow, with a certain humming in my ears,
About the life before I lived this life,
And this life too, popes, cardinals and priests,
Saint Praxed at his sermon on the mount,   95
Your tall pale mother with her talking eyes,
And new-found agate urns as fresh as day,
And marble's language, Latin pure, discreet,
— Aha, ELUCESCBAT[3] quoth our friend?
No Tully, said I, Ulpian at the best!   100
Evil and brief hath been my pilgrimage.
All *lapis*, all, sons! Else I give the Pope
My villas! Will ye ever eat my heart?
Ever your eyes were as a lizard's quick,
They glitter like your mother's for my soul,   105
Or ye would heighten my impoverished frieze,
Piece out its starved design, and fill my vase
With grapes, and add a visor and a Term,[4]
And to the trypod ye would tie a lynx
That in his struggle throws the thyrsus down,   110
To comfort me on my entablature
Whereon I am to lie till I must ask,
"Do I live, am I dead?" There, leave me, there!
For ye have stabbed me with ingratitude
To death — ye wish it — God, ye wish it! Stone —   115
Gritstone, a-crumble! Clammy squares which sweat
As if the corpse they keep were oozing through —
And no more *lapis* to delight the world!
Well, go! I bless ye. Fewer tapers there,
But in a row: and, going, turn your backs   120
— Aye, like departing altar-ministrants,
And leave me in my church, the church for peace,
That I may watch at leisure if he leers —
Old Gandolf — at me, from his onion-stone,
As still he envied me, so fair she was!   125

---

3. he was famous
4. a bust terminating the pedestal

EPILOGUE TO ASOLANDO

At the midnight in the silence of the sleep-time
  When you set your fancies free,
Will they pass to where — by death, fools think, imprisoned —
Low he lies who once so loved you, whom you loved so,
    — Pity me?   5

Oh to love so, be so loved, yet so mistaken!
  What had I on earth to do
With the slothful, with the mawkish, the unmanly?
Like the aimless, helpless, hopeless, did I drivel
    — Being — who?   10

One who never turned his back but marched breast forward,
  Never doubted clouds would break,
Never dreamed, though right were worsted, wrong would triumph,
Held we fall to rise, are baffled to fight better,
    Sleep to wake.   15

No, at noonday in the bustle of man's work-time
  Greet the unseen with a cheer!
Bid him forward, breast and back as either should be,
"Strive and thrive!" cry "Speed, — fight on, fare ever
    There as here!"   20

ARTHUR HUGH CLOUGH (1819-1861)

THE LATEST DECALOGUE

Thou shalt have one God only; who
Would be at the expense of two?
No graven images may be
Worshiped, except the currency:
Swear not at all; for, by thy curse   5
Thine enemy is none the worse:
At church on Sunday to attend
Will serve to keep the world thy friend:
Honor thy parents: that is, all

From whom advancement may befall;   10
Thou shalt not kill; but need'st not strive
Officiously to keep alive:
Do not adultery commit;
Advantage rarely comes of it:
Thou shalt not steal; an empty feat,   15
When it's so lucrative to cheat:
Bear not false witness; let the lie
Have time on its own wings to fly:
Thou shalt not covet, but tradition
Approves all forms of competition.   20

WALT WHITMAN (1819-1892)

FROM *SONG OF MYSELF*

Walt Whitman, a kosmos, of Manhattan the son,
Turbulent, fleshy, sensual, eating, drinking and breeding,
No sentimentalist, no stander above men and women or apart
      from them,
No more modest than immodest.

Unscrew the locks from the doors!   5
Unscrew the doors themselves from their jambs!

Whoever degrades another degrades me,
And whatever is done or said returns at last to me.

Through me the afflatus surging and surging, through me
      the current and index.

I speak the pass-word primeval, I give the sign of democracy,   10
By God! I will accept nothing which all cannot have their
      counterpart of on the same terms.

Through me many long dumb voices,
Vocies of the interminable generations of prisoners and slaves,
Voices of the diseas'd and despairing and of thieves and dwarfs,
Voices of cycles of preparation and accretion,   15

And of the threads that connect the stars, and of wombs and of
    the father-stuff,
And of the rights of them the others are down upon.

* * * * * * * * *

I believe a leaf of grass is no less than the journey-work of
    the stars,
And the pismire[1] is equally perfect, and a grain of
    sand, and the egg of the wren,
And the tree-toad is a chef-d'oevre for the highest,   20
And the running blackberry would adorn the parlors of heaven,
And the narrowest hinge in my hand puts to scorn all
    machinery,
And the cow crunching with depress'd head surpasses any statue,
And a mouse is miracle enough to stagger sextillions of infidels.

* * * * * * * * * *

The spotted hawk swoops by and accuses me, he complains of my   25
    gab and my loitering.

I too am not a bit tamed, I too am untranslatable,
I sound my barbaric yawp over the roofs of the world.

"WHEN I HEARD THE LEARN'D ASTRONOMER"

When I heard the learn'd astronomer,
When the proofs, the figures, were ranged in columns before me,
When I was shown the charts and diagrams, to add, divide,
    and measure them,
When I sitting heard the astronomer where he lectured with
    much applause in the lecture-room,
How soon unaccountable I became tired and sick,   5
Till rising and gliding out I wander'd off by myself,
In the mystical moist night-air, and from time to time,
Look'd up in perfect silence at the stars.

---

1. ant

FROM *WHEN LILACS LAST IN THE DOORYARD BLOOM'D*

Over the breast of the spring, the land, amid cities,
Amid lanes and through old woods, where lately the violets
        peep'd from the ground, spotting the gray debris,
Amid the grass in the fields each side of the lanes, passing
        the endless grass,
Passing the yellow-spear'd wheat, every grain from its shroud
        in the dark-brown fields uprisen,
Passing the apple-tree blows of white and pink in the orchards,   5
Carrying a corpse to where it shall rest in the grave,
Night and day journeys a coffin.

Coffin that passes through lanes and streets,
Through day and night with the great cloud darkening the land,
With the pomp of the inloop'd flags with the cities draped   10
        in black,
With the show of the States themselves as of crape-veil'd
        women standing,
With processions long and winding and the flambeaus of the night,
With the countless torches lit, with the silent sea of faces
        and the unbared heads,
With the waiting depot, the arriving coffin, and the somber
        faces,
With dirges through the night, with the thousand voices rising   15
        strong and solemn,
With all the mournful voices of the dirges pour'd around
        the coffin,
The dim-lit churches and the shuddering organs — where amid
        these you journey,
With the tolling tolling bells' perpetual clang,
Here, coffin that slowly passes,
I give you my sprig of lilac.   20

                *   *   *   *   *   *   *   *   *   *

Lo, body and soul — this land,
My own Manhattan with spires, and the sparkling and hurrying
        tides, and the ships,

The varied and ample land, the South and the North in the
        light, Ohio's shores and flashing Missouri,
And ever the far-spreading prairies cover'd with grass and corn.

Lo, the most excellent sun so calm and haughty,   25
The violet and purple morn with just-felt breezes,
The gentle soft-born measureless light,

The miracle spreading bathing all, the fulfill'd noon,
The coming eve delicious, the welcome night and the stars,
Over my cities shining all, enveloping man and land.   30

MATTHEW ARNOLD (1822-1888)

SHAKESPEARE

Other abide[1] our question, Thou art free.
We ask and ask: thou smilest and art still,
Out-topping knowledge. For the loftiest hill,
Who to the stars uncrowns his majesty,
Planting his steadfast footsteps in the sea,   5
Making the heaven of heavens his dwelling-place,
Spares but the cloudy border of his base
To the foiled searching of mortality;
And thou, who didst the stars and sunbeams know,
Self-schooled, self-scanned, self-honored, self-secure,   10
Didst tread on earth unguessed at. — Better so!
All pains the immortal spirit must endure,
All weakness which impairs, all griefs which bow,
Find their sole speech in that victorious brow.

THE FUTURE

A wanderer is man from his birth.
He was born in a ship
On the breast of the river of Time.
Brimming with wonder and joy
He spreads out his arms to the light,   5
Rivets his gaze on the banks of the stream.

As what he sees is, so have his thoughts been.
Whether he wakes,

---

1. submit to

Where the snowy mountainous pass,
Echoing the screams of the eagles,   10
Hems in its gorges the bed
Of the new-born clear-flowing stream;
Whether he first sees light
Where the river in gleaming rings
Sluggishly winds through the plain;   15
Whether in sound of the swallowing sea —
As is the world on the banks,
So is the mind of the man.

Vainly does each, as he glides,
Fable and dream   20
Of the lands which the River of Time
Had left ere he woke on its breast,
Or shall reach when his eyes have been closed.
Only the tract where he sails
He wots of; only the thoughts,   25
Raised by the objects he passes, are his.

Who can see the green earth any more
As she was by the sources of Time?
Who imagines her fields as they lay
In the sunshine, unworn by the plough?   30
Who thinks as they thought,
The tribes who then lived on her breast,
Her vigorous, primitive sons?

What girl
Now reads in her bosom as clear   35
As Rebekah[2] read, when she sate
At eve by the palm-shaded well?
Who guards in her breast
As deep, as pellucid a spring
Of feeling, as tranquil, as sure?   40

What bard,
At the height of his vision, can deem
Of God, of the world, of the soul,
With a plainness as near,

2.   *Genesis,* xxiv

As flashing as Moses felt,   45
When he lay in the night by his flock
On the starlit Arabian waste?[3]
Can rise and obey
The beck of the Spirit like him?

This tract which the River of Time   50
Now flows through with us, is the plain.
Gone is the calm of its earlier shore.
Bordered by cities, and hoarse
With a thousand cries is its stream.
And we on its breast, our minds   55
Are confused as the cries which we hear,
Changing and shot[4] as the sights which we see.

And we say that repose has fled
For ever the course of the River of Time.
That cities will crowd to its edge   60
In a blacker, incessanter line;
That the din will be more on its banks,
Denser the trade on its stream,
Flatter the plain where it flows,
Fiercer the sun overhead.   65
That never will those on its breast
See an ennobling sight,
Drink of the feeling of quiet again.
But what was before us we know not,
And we know not what shall succeed.   70

Haply, the river of Time,
As it grows, as the towns on its marge
Fling their wavering lights
On a wider, statelier stream —
May acquire, if not the calm   75
Of its early mountainous shore,
Yet a solemn peace of its own.
And the width of the waters, the hush
Of the gray expanse where he floats,
Freshening its current and spotted with foam   80

---

3. *Exodus,* iii
4. variegated

As it draws to the Ocean, may strike
Peace to the soul of the man on its breast —
As the pale waste widens around him —
As the banks fade dimmer away,
As the stars come out, and the night-wind   85
Brings up the stream
Murmurs and scents of the infinite sea.

FROM *RUGBY CHAPEL*

What is the course of the life
Of mortal men on the earth?
Most men eddy about,
Here and there — eat and drink,
Chatter and love and hate,   5
Gather and squander, are raised
Aloft, are hurled in the dust,
Striving blindly, achieving
Nohting; and then they die —
Perish; — and no one asks   10
Who or what they have been,
More than he asks what waves,
In the moonlit solitudes mild
Of the midmost Ocean, have swelled,
Foamed for a moment, and gone.   15

And there are some, whom a thirst
Ardent, unquenchable, fires,
Not with the crowd to be spent,
Not without aim to go round
In an eddy of purposeless dust,   20
Effort unmeaning and vain.
Ah yes! some of us strive
Not without action to die
Fruitless, but something to snatch
From dull oblivion, nor all   25
Glut the devouring grave!

DOVER BEACH

The sea is calm tonight,
The tide is full, the moon lies fair
Upon the straits; on the French coast the light
Gleams and is gone; the cliffs of England stand,
Glimmering and vast, out in the tranquil bay.   5
Come to the window, sweet is the night-air!
Only, from the long line of spray
Where the sea meets the moon-blanched land,
Listen! you hear the grating roar
Of pebbles which the waves draw back, and fling,   10
At their return, up the high strand,
Begin, and cease; and then again begin,
With tremulous cadence slow; and bring
The eternal note of sadness in.

Sophocles, long ago,   15
Heard it on the Aegean, and it brought
Into his mind the turbid ebb and flow
Of human misery; we
Find also in the sound a thought,
Hearing it by this distant northern sea.   20

The Sea of Faith
Was once, too, at the full, and round earth's shore
Lay like the folds of a bright girdle furled;
But now I only hear
Its melancholy long withdrawing roar,   25
Retreating, to the breath
Of the night-wind, down the vast edges drear
And naked shingles of the world.

Ah, love, let us be true
To one another! for the world, which seems   30
To lie before us like a land of dreams,
So various, so beautiful, so new,
Hath really neither joy, nor love, nor light,
Nor certitude, nor peace, nor help for pain;
And we are here as on a darkling plain,   35
Swept with confused alarms of struggle and flight,
Where ignorant armies clash by night.

EMILY DICKINSON (1830-1886)

"THERE'S A CERTAIN SLANT OF LIGHT"

There's a certain slant of light,
On winter afternoons,
That oppresses, like the weight
Of cathedral tunes.

Heavenly hurt it gives us;   5
We can find no scar,
But internal difference
Where the meanings are.

None may teach it anything,
'Tis the seal, despair, —   10
As imperial affliction
Sent us of the air.

When it comes, the landscape listens,
Shadows hold their breath;
When it goes, 'tis like the distance   15
On the look of death.

"I LIKE TO SEE IT LAP THE MILES"

I like to see it lap the miles,
And lick the valleys up,
And stop to feed itself at tanks;
And then, prodigious, step

Around a pile of mountains,   5
And, supercilious, peer
In shanties by the sides of roads;
And then a quarry pare

To fit its sides, and crawl between,
Complaining all the while   10
In horrid, hooting stanza;
Then chase itself downhill

And neigh like Boanerges;
Then, punctual as a star,
Stop—docile and omnipotent—   15
At its own stable door.

"THEY SAY THAT 'TIME ASSUAGES' "

They say that "time assuages," —
    Time never did assuage;
An actual suffering strengthens,
    As sinews do, with age.

Time is a test of trouble,   5
    But not a remedy.
If such it prove, it prove too
    There was no malady.

"HE PREACHED UPON 'BREADTH' "

He preached upon "breadth" till it argued him narrow, —
The broad are too broad to define;
And of "truth" until it proclaimed him a liar, —
The truth never flaunted a sign.

Simplicity fled from his counterfeit presence   5
As gold the pyrites would shun.
What confusion would cover the innocent Jesus
To meet so enabled a man!

"I NEVER SAW A MOOR"

I never saw a moor,
I never saw the sea;
Yet I know how the heather looks,
And what a wave must be.

I never spoke with God,   5
Nor visited in Heaven;
Yet certain am I of the spot
As if the chart were given.

SNAKE

A narrow fellow in the grass
Occasionally rides;
You may have met him, — did you not?
His notice sudden is.

The grass divides as with a comb,   5
A spotted shaft is seen;
And then it closes at your feet
And opens further on.

He likes a boggy acre,
A floor too cool for corn.   10
Yet when a child, and barefoot,
I more than once, at morn,

Have passed, I thought, a whip-lash
Unbraiding in the sun, —
When, stooping to secure it,   15
It wrinkled, and was gone.

Several of nature's people
I know, and they know me;
I feel for them a transport
Of cordiality.   20

But never met this fellow,
Attended or alone,
Without a tighter breathing,
And zero at the bone.

"THERE'S BEEN A DEATH"

There's been a death in the opposite house
    As lately as today.
I know it by the numb look
    Such houses have alway.

The neighbors rustle in and out,   5
    The doctor drives away.
A window opens like a pod,
    Abrupt, mechanically;

Somebody flings a mattress out, —
    The children hurry by;   10
They wonder if It died on that, —
    I used to when a boy.

The minister goes stiffly in
    As if the house were his,
And he owned all the mourners now,   15
    The little boys besides;

And then the milliner, and the man
    Of the appalling trade,
To take the measure of the house,
    There'll be that dark parade

Of tassels and of coaches soon;
    It's easy as a sign, —
The intuition of the news
    In just a country town.

"I DIED FOR BEAUTY"

I died for beauty, but was scarce
Adjusted in the tomb,
When one who died for truth was lain
In an adjoining room.

He questioned softly why I failed?   5
"For beauty," I replied.
"And I for truth, — the two are one;
We brethren are," he said.

And so, as kinsmen met a night,
We talked between the rooms,   10
Until the moss had reached our lips,
And covered up our names.

X

BEGINNINGS OF MODERN POETRY

Every age is "modern" in its own eyes; and so when we speak of Modern Poetry, we must recognize that 100 years hence it will doubtless be classified under terms quite unfamiliar to us. In the context of this text, however, Modern Poetry has in our own time the novel, experimental, adventurous look we think of as "modern."

The reasons that Victorian poets are difficult to classify in any definitive way are even more cogent for poets who come later. The perspective is less, time has done almost nothing to separate the significant from the insignificant, and the English-speaking world continues to grow. (One could, for example, now do a long critical study on an entity as seemingly small as South African literature.) There are literally hundreds of poets presently writing; one cannot begin to read all of them, let alone evaluate them. Any choice of Modern poets — such as that in this anthology — must be regarded as highly tentative: a selection which seemed significant at a given time and place to a given person.

Early Modern Poetry might be said to begin where the Victorian poets ended, and to end with World War I — surely the most devastating event culturally speaking in at least 100 years. Not too surprisingly, Victorian attitudes continued well after the times of Tennyson and Arnold. Thomas Hardy and A. E. Housman, for example, seem to accentuate the mood of "Dover Beach." Hardy's fatalistic philosophy is better known in his novels than in his poetry, but the ideas are substantially the same. Man is a mere pawn in the hands of blind Fate — raised up one day, cast down the next — all for no discoverable reason or purpose. Since the natural world seems to go on, the happiest men are those who live in the simplest, most "natural" fashion, accepting without question whatever comes their way. It is interesting to reflect that a century earlier the Romantic poets also played up the peasantry, but for a rather different reason: Romantic, pre-Darwin nature was a blissful thing, and the closer one could get to it, the more blissful he would be; Hardy's post-Darwin nature, while beautiful in a dark sort of way, was anything but blissful — but by accepting her rhythms of birth and death man could at least endure.

Though Housman wrote far less than Hardy, he had similar ideas. Like Arnold he was a great classical scholar, and doubtless he would have thought of himself more as a teacher than as a poet. For all their somber content his poems have a genial tone to them — a spirit not unlike that of ancient stoicism.

A quality shared by Hardy and Housman is regionalism. Hardy's scene is almost always what he called "Wessex" — roughly the heart of the old Saxon kingdom of that name. Housman writes of Shropshire, a rural county about 100 miles northwest of London. This concentration on a given area is perhaps more common in our age than in previous ones. Yeats sings of Ireland, Frost of New England, Robinson of a small portion of the same, Masters of Illinois. Poets have of course always lived somewhere, and to some extent they have written about that place, but less so in older times. Wordsworth may have been a "Lake Poet," but his specific descriptive pieces range all over Europe, and the Tintern Abbey region is a long way from the Lakes.

Perhaps in a time growing increasingly more complex, dominated by forces increasingly impersonal and beyond control, poets would naturally seek roots somewhere — and roots can only occupy a limited area. In any case, a concentration on a particular locale does appear to be one mark of the Modern.

If we accept Tillich's definition of religion as whatever is of utmost concern, Hardy and Housman, though agnostics, were religious poets. Again not surprisingly, this is one of the marks of the Modern. In a time of violent conflict and shifting values, what does one believe in? The answers are legion, but the question is asked by almost all.

One interesting answer, particularly in Britain, was a revival of traditional religion, particularly Roman Catholicism. Denials of privileges to Roman Catholics ended in the nineteenth century, and so inevitably in its visible form the Church flourished. More important than the visible form was an intellectual revival. In mid-century there began a reform movement within the rather stale Church of England, known as the Oxford Movement. Its many theological ramifications are beyond our scope; very simply it tended to emphasize the "catholic" elements in the Church. For a number of its adherents the movement did not go far enough; the most famous of them, John Henry Newman, became a Roman Catholic and eventually a cardinal.

One response to the increasingly anarchic and fragmented period, then, was the tradition of an ancient faith; and much Modern poetry reflects this response. The late nineteenth century saw two outstanding Roman Catholic poets — Francis Thompson and Gerard Manley Hopkins. In our own time T. S. Eliot, though an Anglican, concentrated on similar points. All three, significantly, are thoroughly Modern; their answer is not to return in some mystical way to the Middle Ages but somehow to relate the broken and meaningless to the unified and meaningful.

One more thing needs to be said about the poets before World War I: some of them experimented in the forms of poetry in ways which we recognize as "different." The trend was not universal: of those we have mentioned, Hardy, Housman, Thompson, Yeats, and Robinson were traditional in form, whatever they may have said. Two nineteenth century figures, however, suggested the directions in form that much later poetry was to take; they were Walt Whitman and G. M. Hopkins.

Whitman thought of himself in self-consciously revolutionary terms: he was to be the prophet of democracy, the poet of the common man.[1] Actually, much that he said was not very revolutionary. His views of nature were not far from those of Emerson, and his political liberalism echoes many a stump speech. He had a certain shock effect, in that he felt that the whole creation was beautiful enough to be celebrated in verse, and hence he rhapsodized about sexual matters in a way that ruffled occasional contemporary feathers. (His comments are pretty tame today.)

What *was* different about Whitman was his form — his style. Most of his poetry lacks rhyme and has no discernible metre; is it then poetry? Too much of it perhaps is not: Whitman is wordy and has a weakness for foreign phrases (sometimes ludicrously misused), grisly malapropisms, and long catalogues of names. At times he reads like the telephone directory. On the other hand, the best of Whitman is unquestionably poetry — a new kind of poetry which has been called *free verse*. While it has no metre, it does have a rhythm — a rising and falling in each line. Whitman modeled it somewhat on the rhythm of the sea: every wave is different from every other wave, yet all have crests and troughs. His verse is also reminiscent of the poetical passages in the King James Bible, which are probably free verse without their writers' knowing it. Whitman felt that a new age called for a new form of writing; his reaction was unquestionably Modern. [Because Whitman chronologically belongs to the mid-nineteenth century, selections from his poetry appear after Chapter IX.]

---

1. Ironically, he has never had much of an audience among common men — even such of them as may occasionally read poetry.

Gerard Manley Hopkins is Modern in a very different way. Where Whitman is diffuse, Hopkins is extremely concentrated; where Whitman reached for something new, Hopkins went back to such ancient traditions that they seemed new.

Hopkins was a fascinating figure: a convert to Roman Catholicism who became a Jesuit monk. He wrote for the glory of God, not for publication; his poems did not appear until the 20's, a generation after his death, when they seemed strikingly original and exciting.

Hopkins's roots were Anglo-Saxon poetry — the language of Beowulf. His experiments were numerous, but one might be mentioned: *sprung rhythm*. In ordinary metrical verse there is a set pattern of stressed and unstressed syllables:

The cúrfew tólls the knéll of párting dáy.

With sprung rhyth,m there are a set number of stressed syllables and *any number* of unstressed one:

The wórld is chárged with the grándeur of Gód,
It will fláme out, like shíning from shóok fóil.

(As one can see, Hopkins also liked alliteration.) Properly read, sprung rhythm is extremely impressive: forceful, varied, exciting. Like free verse, it has been widely used by more recent poets.[2]

---

2. Hopkins actually was not the first to discover sprung rhythm. Coleridge used it in a poem called "Christabel," but his experiment did not then catch on.

THOMAS HARDY (1840-1928)

HAP

If but some vengeful god would call to me
From up the sky, and laugh: "Thou suffering thing,
Know that thy sorrow is my ecstasy,
That they love's loss is my hate's profiting!"
Then would I bear it, clench myself, and die,   5
Steeled by the sense of ire unmerited;
Half-eased in that a Powerfuller than I
Had willed and meted me the tears I shed.

But not so. How arrives it joy lies slain,
And why unblooms the best hope ever sown?   10
— Crass Casualty obstructs the sun and rain,
And dicing Time for gladness casts a moan. . . .
These purblind Doomsters had as readily strown
Blisses about my pilgrimage as pain.

THE DARKLING THRUSH

I leant upon a coppice gate
    When Frost was spectre-gray,
And Winter's dregs made desolate
    The weakening eye of day.
The tangled bine-stems scored the sky   5
    Like strings of broken lyres,
And all mankind that haunted nigh
    Had sought their household fires.

The land's sharp features seemed to be
    The Century's corpse outleant,[1]   10
His crypt the cloudy canopy,
    The wind his death-lament.
The ancient pulse of germ and birth
    Wash shrunken hard and dry,
And every spirit upon earth   15
    Seemed fervorless as I.

---

1. written at the very end of the nineteenth century

At once a voice arose among
    The bleak twigs overhead
In a full-hearted evensong
    Of joy illimited;   20
An aged thrush, frail, gaunt, and small,
    In blast-beruffled plume,
Had chosen thus to fling his soul
    Upon the growing gloom.

So little cause for carolings   25
    Of such ecstatic sound
Was written on terrestrial things
    Afar or nigh around,
That I could think there trembled through
    His happy good-night air   30
Some blessed Hope, whereof he knew
    And I was unaware.

IN TIME OF "THE BREAKING OF NATIONS"[2]

Only a man harrowing clods
    In a slow silent walk
With an old horse that stumbles and nods
    Half asleep as they stalk.

Only thin smoke without flame   5
    From the heaps of couch-grass;
Yet this will go onward the same
    Though Dynasties pass.

Yonder a maid and her wight
    Come whispering by: 10
War's annals will fade into night
    Ere their story die.

2. *Jeremiah*, li, 20

GERARD MANLEY HOPKINS (1844-1889)

GOD'S GRANDEUR

The world is charged with the grandeur of God.
　It will flame out, like shining from shook foil;
　It gathers to a greatness, like the ooze of oil
Crushed. Why do men then now not reck his rod?
Generations have trod, have trod, have trod;　　　　　　　　　　5
　And all is seared with trade, bleared, smeared with toil;
　And wears man's smudge and shares man's smell: the soil
Is bare now, nor can foot feel, being shod.

And for all this, nature is never spent;
　There lives the dearest freshness deep down things;　　　　10
And though the last lights off the black West went
　Oh, morning, at the brokn brink eastward springs—
Because the Holy Ghost over the bent
　World broods with warm breast and with ah! bright wings.

THE WINDHOVER:

To Christ Our Lord

I caught this morning morning's minion, king-
　dom of daylight's dauphin, dapple-dawn-drawn Falcon, in
　　　　his riding
Of the rolling level underneath him steady air, and striding
High there, how he rung upon the rein of a wimpling wing
In his ecstasy! then off, off forth on swing,　　　　　　　　　5
　As a skate's heel sweeps smooth on a bow-bend: the hurl
　　　　and gliding
　Rebuffed the big wind. My heart in hiding
Stirred for a bird, — the achieve of, the mastery of the thing.

Brute beauty and valor and act, oh, air, pride, plume, here
　Buckle! And the fire that breaks from thee then, a billion　　10
Times told lovelier, more dangerous, O my chevalier!

No wonder of it: sheer plot makes plough down sillion[1]
Shine, and blue-break embers, ah my dear,
   Fall, gall themselves, and gash gold-vermillion.

PIED BEAUTY

Glory be to God for dappled things —
   For skies of couple-color as a brinded cow;
     For rose-moles all in stiple upon trout that swim;
Fresh-firecoal chestnut-falls; finches' wings;
   Landscape plotted and pieced — fold, fallow, and plough;   5
   And all trades, their gear and tackle and trim.

All things counter, original, spare, strange;
   Whatever is fickle, freckled (who knows how?)
     With swift, slow; sweet, sour; adazzle, dim;
He fathers-forth whose beauty is past change: 10
       Praise him.

IVERSNAID

   This darksome burn,[2] horseback brown,
   His rollrock highroad roaring down,
   In coop and in comb the fleece of his foam
   Flutes and low to the lake falls home.

   A wind-puff bonnet of fawn-froth.   5
   Turns and twindles over the broth
   Of a pool so pitchblack, fell-frowning,
   It rounds and rounds Despair to drowning.

   Degged with dew, dappled with dew
   Are the groins of the braes that the brook treads through,   10
   Wiry heathpacks, flitches of fern,
   And the beadbonny ash that sits over the burn.

   What would the world be, once bereft
   Of wet and of wildness? Let them be left,
   O let them be left, wildness and wet;   15
   Long live the weeds and the wilderness yet.

---

1. furrow
2. stream

"I WAKE AND FEEL THE FELL OF DARK"

I wake and feel the fell of dark, not day.
What hours, O what black hours have we spent
This night! what sights you, heart, saw; ways you went!
And more must, in yet longer light's delay.
   With witness I speak this. But where I say   5
Hours I mean years, mean life. And my lament
Is cries countless, cries like dead letters sent
To dearest him that lives alas! away.

I am gall, I am heartburn. God's most deep decree
Bitter would have me taste: my taste was me: 10
Bones built in me, flesh filled, blood brimmed the curse.
   Selfyeast of spirit a dull dough sours. I see
The lost are like this, and their scourge to be
As I am mine, their sweating selves; but worse.

ALFRED EDWARD HOUSMAN (1859-1936)

TO AN ATHLETE DYING YOUNG

The time you won your town the race
We chaired you through the market-place;
Man and boy stood cheering by
As home we brought you shoulder-high.

To-day, the road all runners come,   5
Shoulder-high we bring you home,
And set you at your threshold down,
Townsman of a stiller town.

Smart lad, to slip betimes away
From fields where glory does not stay,   10
And early though the laurel grows
It withers quicker than the rose.

Eyes the shady night has shut
Cannot see the record cut,
And silence sounds no worse than cheers   15
After earth has stopped the ears.

Now you will not swell the rout
Of lads that wore their honors out,
Runners whom renown outran
And the name died before the man.   20

So set, before its echoes fade,
The fleet foot on the sill of shade,
And hold to the low lintel up
The still-defended challenge-cup.

And round that early-laurelled head   25
Will flock to gaze the strengthless dead,
And find unwithered on its curls
The garland briefer than a girl's.

"LOVELIEST OF TREES"

Loveliest of trees, the cherry now
Is hung with bloom along the bough,
And stands about the woodland ride,
Wearing white for Eastertide.

Now, of my threescore years and ten,   5
Twenty will not come again,
And take from seventy springs a score,
It only leaves me fifty more.

And since to look at things in bloom
Fifty springs are little room,   10
About the woodlands I will go
To see the cherry hung with snow.

THE CARPENTER'S SON

"Here the hangman stops his cart:
Now the best of friends must part.
Fare you well, for ill fare I;
Live, lads, and I will die.

"Oh, at home had I but stayed   5
'Prenticed to my father's trade,
Had I stuck to plane and adze,
I had not been lost, my lads.

"Then I might have built perhaps
Gallows-trees for other chaps,   10
Never dangled on my own,
Had I but left ill alone.

"Now, you see, they hang me high,
And the people passing by
Stop to shake their fists and curse;   15
So 'tis come from ill to worse.

"Here hang I, and right and left
Two poor fellows hang for theft:
All the same's the luck we prove,
Though the midmost hangs for love.   20

"Comrades all, that stand and gaze,
Walk henceforth in other ways;
See my neck and save your own:
Comrades all, leave ill alone.

"Make some day a decent end,   25
Shrewder fellows than your friend.
Fare you well, for ill fare I:
Live, lads, and I will die."

FRANCIS THOMPSON (1859-1907)

IN NO STRANGE LAND

O world invisible, we view thee,
O world intangible, we touch thee,
O world unknowable, we know thee,
Inapprehensible, we clutch thee!

Does the fish soar to find the ocean,   5
The eagle plunge to find the air —
That we ask of the stars in motion
If they have rumor of thee there?

Not where the wheeling systems darken,
And our benumbed conceiving soars! —   10
The drift of pinions, would we hearken,
Beats at our own clay-shuttered doors.

The angels keep their ancient places; —
Turn but a stone, and start a wing!
'Tis ye, 'tis your estranged faces,   15
That miss the many-splendored thing.

But (when so sad thou canst not sadder)
Cry — and upon thy so sore loss
Shall shine the traffic of Jacob's ladder[1]
Pitched betwixt Heaven and Charing Cross.   20

Yea, in the night, my Soul, my daughter,
Cry — clinging Heaven by the hems;
And lo, Christ walking on the water
Not of Gennesareth, but Thames!

---

1. *Genesis,* xxviii, 11-15

WILLIAM BUTLER YEATS (1865-1939)

THE LAKE ISLE OF INNISFREE

I will arise and go now, and go to Innisfree,
And a small cabin build there, of clay and wattles made:
Nine bean rows will I have there, a hive for the honey-bee,
And live alone in the bee-loud glade.

And I shall have some peace there, for peace comes dropping slow,   5
Dropping from the veils of the morning to where the cricket sings;
There midnight's all a glimmer, and noon's a purple glow,
And evening full of the linnet's wings.

I will arise and go now, for always night and day
I hear lake water lapping with low sounds by the shore;   10
While I stand in the roadway, or on the pavements grey,
I hear it in the deep heart's core.

THE WILD SWANS AT COOLE

The trees are in their autumn beauty,
The woodland paths are dry,
Under the October night the water
Mirrors a still sky;
Upon the brimming water among the stones   5
And nine-and-fifty swans.

The nineteenth autumn has come upon me
Since I first made my count;
I saw, before I had well finished,
All suddenly mount   10
And scatter wheeling in great broken rings
Upon their clamorous wings.

I have looked upon those brilliant creatures,
And now my heart is sore.
All's changed since I, hearing at twilight,   15
The first time on this shore,
The bell-beat of their wings above my head,
Trod with a lighter tread.

Unwearied still, lover by lover,
They paddle in the cold,   20
Companionable streams or climb the air;
Their hearts have not grown old;
Passion or conquest, wander where they will,
Attend upon them still.

But now they drift on the still water   25
Mysterious, beautiful;
Among what rushes will they build,
By what lake's edge or pool
Delight men's eyes when I awake some day
To find they have flown away?   30

WHAT THEN?

His chosen comrades thought at school
He must grow a famous man;
He thought the same and lived by rule,

All his twenties crammed with toil;
"What then?" sang Plato's ghost. "What then?" 5

Everything he wrote was read,
After certain years he won
Sufficient money for his need,
Friends that have been friends indeed;
"What then?" sang Plato's ghost. "What then?" 10

All his happier dreams came true —
A small old house, wife, daughter, son,
Grounds where plum and cabbage grew,
Poets and Wits about him drew;
"What then?" sang Plato's ghost. "What then?" 15

"The work is done," grown old he thought,
"According to my boyish plan;
Let the fools rage, I swerved in naught,
Something to perfection brought";
But louder sang the ghost, "What then?" 20

EDWIN ARLINGTON ROBINSON (1869-1935)

MR. FLOOD'S PARTY

Old Eben Flood, climbing alone one night
Over the hill between the town below
And the forsaken upland hermitage
That held as much as he should ever know
On earth again of home, paused warily. 5
The road was his with not a native near;
And Eben, having leisure, said aloud,
For no men else in Tilbury Town to hear:

"Well, Mr. Flood, we have the harvest moon
Again, and we may not have many more; 10
The bird is on the wing, the poet says,
And you and I have said it here before.
Drink to the bird." He raised up to the light
The jug that he had gone so far to fill,
And answered huskily: "Well, Mr. Flood, 15
Since you propose it, I believe I will."

Alone, as if enduring to the end
A valiant armor of scarred hopes outworn,
He stood there in the middle of the road
Like Roland's ghost winding a silent horn.   20
Below him, in the town among the trees,
Where friends of other days had honored him,
A phantom salutation of the dead
Rang thinly till old Eben's eyes were dim.

Then, as a mother lays her sleeping child   25
Down tenderly, fearing it may awake,
He set the jug down slowly at his feet
With trembling care, knowing that most things break;
And only when assured that on firm earth
It stood, as the uncertain lives of men   30
Assuredly did not, he paced away,
And with his hand extended paused again:

"Well, Mr. Flood, we have not met like this
In a long time; and many a change has come
To both of us, I fear, since last it was   35
We had a drop together. Welcome home!"
Convivially returning with himself,
Again he raised the jug up to the light;
And with an acquiescent quaver said:
"Well, Mr. Flood, if you insist, I might.   40

"Only a very little, Mr. Flood —
For auld lang syne. No more, sir; that will do."
So, for the time, apparently it did,
And Eben evidently thought so too;
For soon amid the silver loneliness   45
Of night he lifted up his voice and sang,
Secure, with only two moons listening,
Until the whole harmonious landscape rang —

"For auld lang syne." The weary throat gave out,
The last word wavered; and the song being done,   50
He raised again the jug regretfully
And shook his head, and was again alone.
There was not much that was ahead of him,

And there was nothing in the town below —
Where strangers would have shut the many doors   55
That many friends had opened long ago.

UNCLE ANANIAS

His words were magic and his heart was true,
    And everywhere he wandered he was blessed.
Of all the ancient men my childhood knew
    I choose him and I mark him for the best.
Of all authoritative liars, too,   5
    I crown him loveliest.

How fondly I remember the delight
    That always glorified him in the spring;
The joyous courage and the benedight
    Profusion of his faith in everything!   10
He was a good old man, and it was right
    That he should have his fling.

And often, underneath the apple-trees,
    When we surprised him in the summer-time,
With what superb magnificence and ease   15
    He sinned enough to make the day sublime!
And if he liked us there about his knees,
    Truly it was no crime.

All summer long we loved him for the same
    Perennial inspiration of his lies;   20
And when the russet wealth of autumn came,
    There flew but fairer visions to our eyes—
Multiple, tropical, winged with a feathery flame,
    Like birds of paradise.

So to the sheltered end of many a year   25
    He charmed the seasons out with pageantry
Wearing upon his forehead, with no fear,
    The laurel of approved iniquity.
And every child who knew him, far or near,
    Did love him faithfully.   30

EDGAR LEE MASTERS (1869-1950)

FROM *SPOON RIVER ANTHOLOGY*

Petit, the Poet

Seeds in a dry pod, tick, tick, tick,
Tick, tick, tick, like mites in a quarrel —
Faint iambics that the full breeze wakens —
But the pine tree makes a symphony thereof.
Triolets, villanelles, rondels, rondeaus,[1]   5
Ballades by the score with the same old thought:
The snows and the roses of yesterday are vanished;
And what is love but a rose that fades?
Life all around me here in the village:
Tragedy, comedy, valor, and truth,   10
Courage, constancy, heroism, failure —
All in the loom, and oh what patterns!
Woodlands, meadows ,streams, and rivers —
Blind to all of it all my life long.
Triolets, villanelles, rondels, rondeaus,   15
Seeds in a dry pod, tick, tick, tick,
Tick, tick, tick, what little iambics,
While Homer and Whitman roared in the pines!

Carl Hamblin

The press of the Spoon River *Clarion* was wrecked
And I was tarred and feathered,
For publishing this on the day the Anarchists were hanged
          in Chicago:
"I saw a beautiful woman with bandaged eyes
Standing on the steps of a marble temple.   5
Great multitudes passed in front of her,
Lifting their faces to her imploringly.
In her left hand she held a sword.
She was brandishing the sword,
Sometimes striking a child, again a laborer,   10
Again a slinking woman, again a lunatic.
In her right hand she held a scale;
Into the scales pieces of gold were tossed
By those who dodged the strokes of the sword.

---

1. several very conventional types of verse

A man in a black gown read from a manuscript: 15
'She is no respecter of persons.'
Then a youth wearing a red cap
Leaped to her side and snatched away the bandage.
And lo, the lashes had been eaten away
From the oozy eye-lids;   20
The eye-balls were seared with a milky mucus;
The madness of a dying soul
Was written on her face —
But the multitude saw why she wore the bandage."

Seth Compton

When I died, the circulating library
Which I built up for Spoon River,
And managed for the good of inquiring minds,
Was sold at auction on the public square,
As if to destroy the last vestige   5
Of my memory and influence.
For those of you who could not see the virtue
Of knowing Volney's "Ruins" as well as Butler's "Analogy"
And "Faust" as well as "Evangeline,"
Were really the power in the village,   10
And often you asked me,
"What is the use of knowing the evil in the world?"
I am out of your way now, Spoon River,
Choose your own good and call it good.
For I could never make you see   15
That no one knows what is good
Who knows not what is evil;
And no one knows what is true
Who knows not what is false.

Anne Rutledge

Out of me unworthy and unknown
The vibrations of deathless music;
"With malice toward none, with charity for all."
Out of me the forgiveness of millions toward millions,
And the beneficent face of a nation   5
Shining with justice and truth.
I am Anne Rutledge who sleep beneath these weeds,

Beloved in life of Abraham Lincoln,
Wedded to him, not through union,
But through separation.   10
Bloom forever, O Republic,
From the dust of my bosom!

XI

POETRY SINCE WORLD WAR I

Any discussion of human activity since World War I must consider the supreme importance of the war itself. Far more than most dates, 1914 marks the end of one age and the beginning of a very different one.

The most obvious reason for this was the sheer magnitude and destructiveness of the conflict. Casualties were staggering. France lost about 10% of her male population — the most vigorous 10%, at its most vigorous time of life. (If the United States today should suffer somewhat more than 10,000,000 killed in action in a war — all young men — the loss would be proportional.) United States losses were minute by comparison, but Britain suffered heavily — and because she relied in the early years on volunteers, it was the most patriotic and high-minded group that was not around when the war was over.

Less horrible but still appalling casualties were material: the land of France, the ships of Britain, the financial stability of practically every country involved.

Secondly, the war shocked because Europe more or less blundered into it, quite unaware of what it was getting into. The fumbling of diplomats in 1914 now reads like a Greek tragedy, and the young men who rushed to the colors thought they were off to high adventure. After all, hardly anyone in Europe was familiar with modern war; there hadn't been a major war involving a "civilized" country for a long time. By the time the full horror of the trenches became obvious to all, there was no pulling out till one side gave up.

Finally, one can think of no wars where the results were so far from the objectives. Woodrow Wilson, no mean phrase-maker, summed up American war aims in a famous slogan. It would "make the world safe for democracy." The British called it "the war to end wars." The statements were sincerely made, and millions endured suffering buoyed by them. Then, what happened? There has been some sort of war somewhere ever since the "war to end wars" — in fact World War II in considerable measure grew out of it. And universal democracy looked far safer in 1914 than in 1919. The United States, to cite one example, went from the Progressive Era to Warren Gamaliel Harding.

The reaction following World War I, then, was far greater than that following most wars — certainly greater than that following the slogan-less, banner-less, song-less World War II.[1]

The times of violence and discord unleashed by World War I could not help but influence poets — but in so many ways that no short summary could possibly really summarize. Rather than more or less list the various poetical reactions, we shall consider just two poets, quite different from one another but about as sure of a permanent place in literature as the modern commentator dares to say.

Robert Frost is the first. Superficially, he is a homespun lover of the New England scene; or perhaps a cracker-barrel philosopher sitting beside the stove in the village store. The superficial is of course partly true, but it leaves out the important Frost. In his laconic Yankee way he is a crusader for the worth of the individual. One kind of individualism is the crusty New Hampshire or Vermont farmer type that one sees in the superficial Frost. But in poem after poem he also asserts the supreme importance of the individual in a mass-produced, computerized world. He once objected to the customary pronunciation of the title of one of his poems. "It's not 'The Death of the *Hired* Man'," he said, "but 'The Death of the Hired *Man*.' " On another occasion he stated that "brain-wash," a word we use so casually, was the ugliest word he'd ever heard. Frost's insistence on personal worth and integrity is one of the major marks of Modern Poetry.

Frost's poetry is traditional in form — perhaps in itself a mark of his individualism. He felt that writing free verse was like playing tennis with the net down. In his discipline and craftsmanship Robert Frost was very much the man of dignity which his poetry suggested was vital to the time.

Also in Frost one finds skepticism — a healthy attitude in revolutionary times. Most people are either unthinking believers or cynics — and sometimes both at the same time. They are too easily shown or they can't be shown at all. Robert Frost questions, but he's willing to be shown.

Another recent poet of almost certain permanence is Thomas Stearns Eliot. He is superficially more difficult than Frost: he relies heavily on symbolic language, made particularly difficult because of his

---

1. There really was only one "soldiers' song" in the United States Army during World War II, and that was "Lili Marlene," a ballad about a prostitute swiped from the Germans!

enormous erudition; he moves from point to point in the manner of *stream of consciousness* rather than logical structure; and he specifically tackles major philosophical problems, which Frost is likely to hint at.

Eliot is noted for his startling technique; he is quite obviously "modern" in form, though disciplined at the same time, and well aware (like Hopkins) of the importance of tradition. He is probably most important, however, for what might be called his "spiritual autobiography," which came out over the years in a series of memorable poems. There was despair in the 20's with "The Waste Land" and "The Hollow Men." Then came the steep cliff out of the mire: "Ash Wednesday" and "Journey of the Magi." Finally, the "Four Quartets" are profound statements of faith.

For Eliot, the faith was traditional Christianity, to which he became converted. Perhaps not every man can find his way as Eliot did; but the body of his poetry is a testament that even twentieth century man — and no one was more so than Eliot — can find "the still point of the turning world." Both he and Frost testify to the importance that man do so.

ROBERT FROST (1875-1963)

THE ROAD NOT TAKEN

Two roads diverged in a yellow wood,
And sorry I could not travel both
And be one traveler, long I stood
And looked down one as far as I could
To see where it bent in the undergrowth;

Then took the other, as just as fair,
But having perhaps the better claim,
Because it was grassy and wanted wear;
Though as for that the passing there
Had worn them really about the same.   10

And both that morning equally lay
In leaves no step had trodden black.
Oh, I kept the first for another day!
Yet knowing how way leads on to way,
I doubted if I should ever come back.   15

I shall be telling this with a sigh
Somewhere ages and ages hence:
Two roads diverged in a wood, and I —
I took the one less traveled by,
And that has made all the difference.   20

FIRE AND ICE

Some say the world will end in fire,
Some say in ice.
From what I've tasted of desire
I hold with those who favor fire.
But if it had to perish twice,   5
I think I know enough of hate
To say that for destruction ice
Is also great
And would suffice.

STOPPING BY WOODS ON A SNOWY EVENING

Whose woods these are I think I know.
His house is in the village though;
I will not see me stopping here
To watch his woods fill up with snow.

My little horse must think it queer   5
To stop without a farmhouse near
Between the woods and frozen lake
The darkest evening of the year.

He gives his harness bells a shake
To ask if there is some mistake.   10
The only other sound's the sweep
Of easy wind and downy flake.

The woods are lovely, dark and deep.
But I have promises to keep,
And miles to go before I sleep.   15
And miles to go before I sleep.

"TREE AT MY WINDOW"

Tree at my window, window tree,
My sash is lowered when night comes on;
But let there never be curtain drawn
Between you and me.

Vague dream-head lifted out of the ground,   5
And thing next most diffuse to cloud,
Not all your light tongues talking aloud
Could be profound.

But, tree, I have seen you taken and tossed,
And if you have seen me when I slept,   10
You have seen me when I was taken and swept
And all but lost.

The day she put our heads together,
Fate had her imagination about her,
Your head so much concerned with outer,   15
Mine with inner, weather.

THOMAS STEARNS ELIOT (1888-1964)

THE HOLLOW MEN

A penny for the Old Guy[1]

I

We are the hollow men
We are the stuffed men
Leaning together
Headpiece filled with straw. Alas!
Our dried voices, when
We whisper together
Are quiet and meaningless
As wind in dry grass

Or rats' feet over broken glass
In our dry cellar.   10

Shape without form shade without color,
Paralyzed force, gesture without motion;

Those who have crossed
With direct eyes, to death's other Kingdom
Remember us — if at all — not as lost   15
Violent souls,[2] but only
As the hollow men
The stuffed men.

II

Eyes I dare not meet in dreams
In death's dream kingdom   20
These do not appear:
There, the eyes are
Sunlight on a broken column
There, a tree swinging
And voices are   25
In the wind's singing
More distant and more solemn
Than a fading star.

---

1. Traditional children's cry in Britain on Guy Fawkes Day (November 5). The "Old Guy" is a stuffed replica of Fawkes.
2. In contrast, Fawkes was executed for trying to blow up Parliament.

Let me be no nearer
In death's dream kingdom   30
Let me also wear
Such delibate disguises
Rat's skin, crowskin, crossed staves
In a field
Behaving as the wind behaves   35
No nearer —

Not that final meeting
In the twilight kingdom.

III

This is the dead land
This is cactus land   40
Here the stone images
Are raised, here they receive
The supplication of a dead man's hand
Under the twinkle of a fading star.

Is it like this   45
In death's other kingdom
Waking alone
At the hour when we are
Trembling with tenderness
Lips that would kiss   50
Form prayers to broken stone.

IV

The eyes are not here
There are no eyes here
In this valley of dying stars
In this hollow valley   55
This broken jaw of our lost kingdoms

In this last of meeting places
We grope together
And avoid speech
Gathered on this beach of the tumid river   60

Sightless, unless
The eyes reappear
As the perpetual star
Multifoliate rose
Of death's twilight kingdom   65
The hope only
Of empty men.

                              V
Here we go round the prickly pear
Prickly pear prickly pear
Here we go round the prickly pear   70
At five o'clock in the morning.

Betwen the idea
And the reality
Between the motion
And the act   75
Falls the Shadow
                    For Thine is the Kingdom

Between the conception
And the creation
Between the emotion   80
And the response
Falls the Shadow
                              Life is very long

Between the desire
And the spasm   85
Between the potency
And the existence
Between the essence
And the descent
Falls the Shadow   90
                    For Thine is the Kingdom

For Thine is
Life is
For Thine is the

This is the way the world ends   95
This is the way the world ends
This is the way the world ends
Not with a bang but a whimper.

JOURNEY OF THE MAGI

"A cold coming we had of it,
Just the worst time of the year
For a journey, and such a long journey:
The ways deep and the weather sharp,
The very dead of winter."[3]   5
And the camels galled, sore-footed, refractory,
Lying down in the melting snow
There were times we regretted
The summer palaces on slopes, the terraces,
And the silken girls bringing sherbet.   10
Then the camel men cursing and grumbling
And running away, and wanting their liquor and women,
And the night-fires going out, and the lack of shelters,
And the cities hostile and the towns unfriendly
And the villages dirty and charging high prices: 15
A hard time we had of it.
At the end we preferred to travel all night,
Sleeping in snatches,
With the voices singing in our ears, saying
That this was all folly.   20

Then at dawn we came down to a temperate valley,
Wet, below the snow line, smelling of vegetation;
With a running stream and a water-mill beating the darkness,
And three trees on the low sky,
And an old white horse galloped away in the meadow.   25
Then we came to a tavern with vine-leaves over the lintel,
Six hands at an open door dicing for pieces of silver,
And feet kicking the empty wine-skins.
But there was no information, and so we continued

---

3. The quotation is from Bishop Lancelot Andrewes (1555-1626), a
   noted scholar of his time and the leader of the group appointed to
   make the King James translation of the Bible.

And arrived at evening, not a moment too soon   30
Finding the place; it was (you may say) satisfactory.

All this was a long time ago, I remember,
And I would do it again, but set down
This set down
This: were we led all that way for   35
Birth or Death? There was a Birth, certainly,
We had evidence and no doubt. I had seen birth and death,
But had thought they were different; this Birth was
Hard and bitter agony for us, like Death, our death.
We returned to our places, these Kingdoms,   40
But no longer at ease here, in the old dispensation,
With an alien people clutching their gods.
I should be glad of another death.

INDEX OF AUTHORS